Women in Management

The ITT Key Issues Lecture Series

is made possible through a grant from
International Telephone and Telegraph Corporation

This series of lectures took place
from December 1979 to April 1980
at Simmons College
in Boston, Massachusetts

Women in Management

Edited by
Milton L. Shuch
Simmons College

With a foreword by
Rand V. Araskog

Bobbs-Merrill Educational Publishing
Indianapolis

The Bobbs-Merrill Company, Inc.
4300 West 62nd Street
Indianapolis, Indiana 46268
First Edition
First Printing 1981

Library of Congress Cataloging in Publication Data
Main entry under title:

Women in management.

(ITT key issues lecture series)
    Contents: Blueprint for the top manager—
me / Polly Bergen—Personal economics for
today's woman / Sylvia Auerbach—Communi-
cating and managing the media challenge /
Lenore Hershey—[etc.]
    1. Women executives—Addresses, essays,
lectures. I. Shuch, Milton L.
HF5500.2.W66   658'.0088042   81-6120
ISBN 0-672-97919-5   AACR2

Contents

Foreword

Rand V. Araskog

Chairman and President
International Telephone and Telegraph Corporation

Our economic world has been fortunate to see in recent years the ever-increasing presence of women in management. According to the Equal Employment Opportunity Commission, for the period 1970–1978, the number of women managers and officers in U.S. corporations with more than 100 employees rose to 601,000 from 261,000.

This fact is indicative of the great unreported middle ground that exists in management today, where thousands of women are being given appropriate training and well-deserved promotions. I think this steady advancement in women's professional status is much more significant than the unfortunate exceptions which capture the headlines from time to time.

Barbara Franklin of the University of Pennsylvania describes in Chapter 4 how women are being recruited for top policy-making jobs in government. For example, in 1970, less than 5 percent of our foreign service officer corps was female. How-

ever, by 1979, women constituted 11.5 percent of that elite
group. Female representation at the junior officer level also
more than doubled over an 8-year period, to 20 percent from 9
percent.

Lenore Hershey of the *Ladies' Home Journal* stresses in Chapter
3 the need to establish priorities. With this I heartily concur.
Further, all of us in management have a duty to help motivate
young people to pursue careers in business.

For his splendid support, we are grateful to Dr. Milton L.
Shuch, Chairman of the Department of Management at Simmons, who organized the series and edited this volume. And
special thanks are due the six participants who brought their individual experience and their personal style to the Boston
campus.

But I was most encouraged by the hundreds of women, of all
ages, who attended these lectures. Their searching questions af-
forded evidence of women's desire and determination to attain
full partnership status in business.

Introduction

Milton L. Shuch

Since 1974 Milton L. Shuch has served as Associate Professor of Retailing and Director of the Prince Program in Retailing at Simmons College in Boston. From 1976 to 1980 he was also Chairman of the Department of Management. Before coming to Simmons, he was Assistant Professor in Marketing and Retailing at Nassau Community College in Garden City, New York.

Professor Shuch received his B.S. in Marketing from Hofstra University; he earned his M.A. in Business Education and his Ph.D. in Administration of Business Education in Higher Education from New York University. From 1952 to 1968 he owned and operated a chain of women's ready-to-wear shops which employed approximately sixty people.

Although the articles in this book are written by women, the lessons to be learned have value for both sexes. As men have been dominant for so long, they may have developed a myopic view of the road to success. This is not to say that men are unwilling to help and share, but they may not recognize how to render assistance and in what areas.

Undoubtedly, too, there is prejudice against women; and, where bias is present, these articles may help some open-minded men to understand the hurdles women must overcome. At best, these men will become advocates, but minimally there may be an attitudinal change away from obstructionism.

Writers at some future time will be in a better position to give an analysis of women in management. At this point, it appears that the topic has very limited relative perspective, for we are too close to what may be the real beginning of the women's movement. Further, the impact that women have had on management as a field and within specific areas is too limited to assess. A fair evaluation can be accomplished only when a larger body of women have had the same managerial opportunities as men and for a time period of sufficient duration.

There is little doubt that the number of women who are filtering upward through the ranks to top management positions is on the increase. However, as the articles in this book point out, there are too few.

The purpose of this series of articles is to identify, to the extent possible, the working environment, character, and background associated with different areas of management. The participants have been candid, have given us personal glimpses into their makeup, and have started to identify desirable and unacceptable traits for women managers.

Some of the contributors to this book have, through sheer coincidence, identified similar issues and problems; in other instances, the authors have generated individual views of a question. The similarities are undoubtedly due to the fact that all of the writers are women who have experienced comparable difficulties and successes in their careers. The differences expressed by these women are to some extent a function of their diverse professions, but more important is the fact that each of them is an individual.

Polly Bergen's essay concludes with the admonition that women should strive to be originals and not copies. Perhaps this is one of the major lessons to be learned, and it certainly is not one for women alone. Our free-enterprise society is founded on the theory that rewards are available to anyone with the strength, knowledge, ability, and determination to do and be something different. Bergen's statement is, then, both a reminder and a pointed reproach to women who may seek success through imitation rather than by striking out and making their own individualistic statement.

All of the authors in this book are unique and talented women, who have made their mark in different fields and by dissimilar routes. They discuss subjects such as power—obtaining it, using it, and relinquishing it; what women can expect to need in terms of education, both formally and through work experience; raising a family and the implications for a profession; conditioning; dealing with men; and responsibilities of employers, the government, and society in general.

Do the writers feel the pathways to success are easier now; is prejudice less; are opportunities increasing? All of the women are enthusiastic about the outlook. They are positive in their thinking about themselves and the prospects for others.

Women in Management

ONE

Blueprint for the

Top Manager—*Me*

Polly Bergen

Polly Bergen is an award-winning actress, recording star, author, mother, humanitarian, and businesswoman. In this last role she is a director of the Singer Company—the first woman director in the company's 124-year history. At Singer she serves as chairwoman of the Marketing Committee and also as a member of the Finance Committee.

At one point in my life, which was more recent than it should have been, I discovered that the most important skill I had to develop was the ability to manage myself.

At the time, I owned and ran my own cosmetics company; and, of course, everyone was very interested in beauty and cosmetics and hair and fashions. I was often called upon to address very large groups of women. I'd always get enormously insecure and immediately rush out to buy a new outfit. It had to be something very special, something that I would be reasonably

1

certain no one else in the audience would have. (It would be a Loretta Young entrance dress—for those of you who remember Loretta Young! For the rest of you, it was a Cher entrance dress, maybe a little more concealing.) I would walk out on stage, and my opening remark would always be, "How do you like my outfit?" Then I would turn, and everyone would applaud. Somehow, I remember, that would give me a sense of security, a feeling that the audience had approved of me; and I could more or less go on with what it was I had to say. Well, I still start my lectures by saying, "How do you like my outfit?" And I still turn. The difference, however, is that I now say, "Thank you very much" but don't really care whether my outfit is liked or not! If there's one feeling I'd like you to develop it is not to care if the people around you like your outfit. I think that if my remarks have a particular thrust, it is that from now on you should do nothing—nothing in your life—that does not make you feel good about you.

It's interesting: all of us suffer from conditioning. I've discovered that whether you were born in the thirties, the forties, the fifties, or the sixties, there really has been no change. Oh, perhaps there have been a few changes; but all of us still have a certain amount of conditioning. It's something we're not aware of, it's something our families are not aware of, it's something that most people never really give a thought to. It is (I may have created this word, I'm not sure) a *genderization* of living. It is the feeling that we must always do what is expected of us. We must always be approved of. We spend our lives getting "yes votes" from everyone. This is true for men as well as for women, for they must deal with "genderization," too. They are trapped very early in life with the problem of being drilled that they must grow up, they must pick a profession in which they will be successful, they must be successful in it, they must be the breadwinner, they must make sure they can buy the house and the car and take care of the wife and send the children to college and have the ability to pay for a certain number of vacations. Consequently, there are men today who, by the millions, tramp to and from work they despise because they chose to do that which would give them some semblance of respectability or professionalism or a steady income or a chance to get rich. But, by and large, at that particular point, the conditioning that runs their lives stops. They acquire a certain amount of control from then on.

We women, on the other hand (and I don't care how recently we were born, and I don't care what we've read and what we've learned with the emergence of the Women's Movement), somewhere in the back of our heads have the idea that we are going to grow up, and we are going to meet this terrific guy who has been trained to take care of us, and we are going to get married, and we are going to have kids. We are never going to have to worry about anything, because he's going to worry. The truth? Now, of course, we have a double vision, you see. Now we've really got it all made because we can be career women, we can go out and be fabulous and do everything we want to do, but somewhere in our heads we're still saying, "Hey, we'll find this guy who will take care of us." Right?

So we spend our lives—we women, anyway—seeking "yes votes." Very important, because, you see, basically we're only as pretty as our husbands or our boyfriends tell us we are; only as bright as our bosses tell us we are; only as sexy as our husbands or boyfriends (or both, depending on lifestyle) tell us we are; only as good a mother as our children tell us we are; only as intelligent, as giving, as much a humanitarian as our friends and neighbors tell us we are. We go through life gathering all these "yes votes"; and we're content because our children tell us we're good mothers, our husbands tell us we're beautiful, and our bosses tell us we're bright. Now, if we're really lucky, we may go through all of our lives with that support system—which would be terrific. There may be moments of anxiety, moments when for a flash something intrudes and makes us feel a little scared, but only moments. There's only one problem with the system. Our children grow up; and if we've trained them properly, and given them the kind of sense of themselves that we hope to give, they will go out into the world and form lives of their own. Oh, they won't stop loving us, they will continue to love us; they will occasionally see us, we'll hear from them ("Hello, Mom, could I borrow $10?"). But they really won't be there all the time, saying,

"Gee, you're a terrific mother," or "Gee, you're a terrific father."

Now statistically (I don't mean to lay this on you guys) we out-live you. We do outlive you. What I'm really trying to say, and it's as important a message for the men as it is for the women, is this: we, as women, ultimately end up alone. It's kind of a scary word, *alone*. It's an awful word, *alone!* Because, when you are alone, you are with you. So, why is that scary? Why are you so terrified? Because, for the first time, you have to look at your feelings about you. There isn't a support system standing around you, telling you how terrific you are. You are stuck with how you really feel about you. And most of us stop looking at that after the first ten or twelve or fifteen or maybe eighteen years of our lives. We allow the support system to take over, and it adds insulation, layer on top of layer on top of layer over our true feelings about ourselves. So, we ultimately think insecurity has disappeared.

Well, one morning I woke up at the age of forty-one, and I was alone. (This was the point in time to which I referred at the beginning of this essay.) I had been married twenty-five years, I had three children who were comparatively grown-up, and I was alone.

Polly Bergen—people have an image of who that is, I guess: sure, capable, successful, certainly able to earn her own living, attractive, strong. I have never been so scared. There was a period of time when I really wasn't sure I was going to continue to survive. I suddenly realized that this wonderful identification that I sincerely believed was me, as did everyone else, was just a lot of layers that I had acquired, and that, in reality, I had not changed at all from the time I was a little girl.

Of course, it really came home the first Christmas that I was alone: I called the children and asked them to spend the holidays with me (we had always gone to Acapulco for Christmases and New Years). The kids said, "Sure, Mom," and off we traipsed to Acapulco. I remember sitting on the beach in my back-too-short, watching all the gorgeous nineteen-year-olds go by in bikinis, and saying, "Bury me in the sand, please God"—but she didn't. I remember going home, climbing up the stairs, sitting down, looking into the mirror, and realizing suddenly that I was looking at the same face and the same body that I had looked at when I was eleven years old. It was a fascinating thing to see.

You see, when I was eleven, I was my full height, which is 5 feet 5½ inches, and I weighed about 155 pounds. I had a 40-inch hip and a 40-inch bust, which is terrific when you're twenty-five but really gets in the way a lot when you're eleven. I flunked Physical Education three years in a row because I would not get undressed in front of the other girls. I remember the dances particularly, on Saturday night in the gym. All the girls would line up on one side of the gym, and all the guys would line up on the other side. You would sort of show up and do all of the steps. One of the guys would say, "Not bad," and he'd come over and tap you on the shoulder. There was an unwritten law in those days, Tall Person Leads. Well, I was the tallest person in my class, taller than anyone three classes ahead of me, so, consequently, to this day when I walk out on a dance floor, within three minutes the guy will stop and say, "Okay, are you gonna lead, or am I gonna lead?" It's very strange how that conditioning in your early years stays with you. I had this image of myself that was a nightmare: I never got invited to any of the proms, I was this wonderful kind of grotesque elephant/giraffe. That's the closest I can come.

At the age of eighteen people caught up with me; there were suddenly men taller than me—and there were a couple of girls taller than me. I had lost a little weight, too, but I still had fat feelings in the back of my head, this lovely picture of an elephant/giraffe. The fact that Jane Powell was my very first friend in show business did not help, because Jane Powell is 2 feet 7 inches and weighs 23 pounds. Neither did the fact that my second best friend in show business was Elizabeth Taylor, who would wake up at five o'clock in the morning on a camping trip and be so beautiful you wanted to stab her in the chest with a fork!

But in spite of all these problems I continued to strive. I probably tried harder—because I felt I had all of these terrible problems to overcome. Ultimately, there was a certain amount of success. I learned how to dress and put myself together; and soon I had acquired enough layers truly to believe that I had changed, that I was this tall, slim, beautiful, elegant, successful, intelligent woman. Until I woke up that morning alone. Then I looked in the mirror, and I saw that elephant/giraffe. I realized something at that moment—that was the beginning of the most important lesson I ever had to learn, which is that ultimately we all must take the responsibility for ourselves. Ultimately, we must look at how we feel about who we are, because that's who we really live with. That is the nucleus of our identity, and that will always be there, no matter how many "yes votes" we get. It will always be in the way, no matter what we do, because that is who we really are. Everything else is play-acting.

Play-acting was very easy for me, because that happened to be the way I earned my living. The fact that the play-acting continued when I went home was something I wasn't aware of. The fact that I lived with it year after year after year was something I wasn't aware of. I suddenly realized that I was going to have to grow up—and it's embarrassing to have to start to grow up when you're forty-one years old. I suddenly realized that this brilliant, wonderful woman who had built this company and was running it by herself, who could add the figures up faster than they could punch them out on the little computer, didn't know how to pay her own insurance, didn't know how to mortgage a house or arrange car payments, had never once taken the responsibility for herself; that was *his* job. *He* was supposed to be my husband and my lover and my accountant, my provider and my doctor and my lawyer and Indian chief. A lot of pressure to put on somebody, isn't it? A lot of power to give somebody, isn't it? Because, you see, it's wonderful, in a way; then whatever happens, it's his fault, He did it. I would have saved the money, but he did it. He was in charge of investing, he did it. No, you did it. You did it, you made the choice not to be a partner. And you made him say, "No, honey, I'll take care of it"; you made the choice not to be a partner. People don't take power, you give it. You give the other person power. You give the boss power. You give your friends power to hurt you, to do you wrong. That is a choice, a choice *you* make. It is not something *they* do.

Taking over responsibility for someone else is a fairly difficult thing to do; it is a very dangerous thing to do. Taking the responsibility for oneself is even more difficult, but it is not dangerous. Yes, you will suddenly become responsible for all your own failures, but you will also become responsible for your own successes. I never once gave myself credit for anything I did in my life. I always thought that somebody else was responsible for it. If I did a terrific acting job in something, it wasn't me, it was that I was lucky enough to get this brilliant director. If I walked into a business meeting and I managed to work my way through that business meeting and get everything that I needed to have for my business, and the other person would be shaking his or her head and saying, "Boy, you're a tough negotiator, that's terrific," I would walk out and say, "Whew, I fooled one more person." I fooled one more person. What you create is this twenty-four-hour-a-day fear that someone is going to find you out, someone is going to discover that you really aren't smart, that you are just fooling, that you are winging it. I winged it—I got through that examination by winging it; I don't really know it, I just crammed and I did it. But, you know, I don't really know. So, there's never any joy at success, because it's not yours. You didn't really do it, you faked it and you got lucky. It was not really your failure—from which you could learn, because I've learned more from my failures than I have from my successes—because it was the other person's. They did something that made it not work, you didn't do it. How could you do it: if you're incapable of being successful, how could you be capable of failing?

I tried a very interesting exercise, an exercise that I went into because I felt that I had to start somewhere, and I didn't know where to start, quite honestly. But I knew that somewhere, tied up in me, there was an awful lot of ego about the way I looked. And I knew that, while everybody says it's what's inside that counts (I *know* it's what's inside that counts), the major problem is that, from fifty feet away, it's tough to see what's inside. The fact is, we live in a visual society, where each and every one of us makes an instant judgment, whether we admit it or not, an instant judgment on every person we see by what we see: by their color, by their height, by their weight, by their clothing, by their skin, by their hair. I have a secret little criterion: I judge all guys by their heels. If they're rundown heels, that means he's either very, very rich or a bum. I'm kidding, but it is true. It's an instant judgment. Long before you discover that people are wonderful, before they have an opportunity to show you how bright they are or how nice they are, how dear they are or how loving they are, you've made this judgment on the physical.

So what I did is something very interesting: I stood in front of a full-length mirror with a lot of bright lights on, I removed all my clothing, and I then put on my glasses. Do you know how many people hide behind clothing? It's funny, really. At a reception recently, I was saying, "Oh, I shouldn't eat that because, you know, I've got to lose five pounds." Another woman guest said, "You look wonderful." I said, "Do you think I'm a dummy? I know how to dress so I look wonderful." I mean, I know how to do that. How many of you have recently removed all of your clothing and looked at yourself in a brightly lit mirror? Did certain things become obvious to you immediately? Now, I value my job, but I had somehow, without even knowing, added one pound a year for every year I had been married. It was like a gift I gave myself—whew, got through another year, I can put on a pound. It was a giving way, because I had this situation so much in control that I didn't have to worry about it any more. So I had just stopped looking, but the fact was, you see, I knew what was underneath that clothing. I knew, like going nude today. Remember what I said earlier? What makes you feel good about you? You see, 1,200 people can say to me, "But you're perfect, you don't need to lose weight." But I know what's underneath! Now, it's my reaction to it, *mine,* that is important. This exercise is a very important one. When we look in the mirror, it is our reaction to us, not "What do you think Harriet will say?" or "Do you think Al will like this?" How do you feel about what you see? It is my firm belief that the *physical* is as much a part of the *pretend* as anything else. The way we react to ourselves physically is as much a part of who we are as how we react to what's inside.

I took a pad and a pencil and I drew a line down the middle of the pad; on the right side of the pad I wrote down all the things I liked about myself and on the left side of the pad I wrote down all the things I hated about myself. I was really glad that I had used a legal pad because the list got long. The next thing I did was look down the list of things I hated about myself and zero in on each and every one of those things I could not change. Do you know how much time we spend making ourselves crazy over things we cannot change? Has anybody recently realized that if you wrote down on that left side of the page, I am sixty-two, you would still be sixty-three next year? I remember writing down particularly, "I hate my legs." I am 5 feet 5½ inches tall, 5 feet 5 inches of which is body and one-half inch of which is legs. I have gone to twenty-seven plastic surgeons who have told me they cannot put an insert between my knees and ankles. I've done everything I could to disguise the fact that I have these short, stumpy legs; I never wear things that are a different color from top to bottom. That way, you don't know where my legs begin. I always wear three-inch heels to give my legs more length. (It looks a little silly when I'm naked, and gets in the way in the bed, but I hang in on that!) Now someone is thinking, "I don't think her legs look so bad." I don't care what you think about my legs; I hate my legs! Have I made my point?

What you're going to do is, you're going to deal with each one of those things you can change. You are not going to waste another moment in your life thinking about, worrying about, being driven crazy about those things you cannot change. You're going to deal with each one of them psychologically. Each one of them, you're going to come to terms with. I drew a line through that particular sentence and said, "I will never refer again to my legs as short and stumpy; I happen to think I have terrific legs." Of course, I still wear three-inch heels. And after "I am forty-one years old," I wrote, "Probably the best forty-one-year-old you ever saw." And I went down the line. Now on to those things I could change. How badly did I want to change them? How important were they to the feelings I had about myself? (When I say "I," I hope you're thinking "me," because that's what you're supposed to be doing. I'm saying "I" because everything I'm saying is what I have fought my way through, and what I have a feeling most of you have fought or will fight your way through.) Now, there may be a few of you who have trouble gaining weight, and if you do, your problem isn't very much different.

You see, the fact is that from the age of thirty-five on, you will be on a diet for the rest of your life.

Now, I'm only going to bring that up for one very simple reason, because we are now going to get into the area of common sense: *common* sense. Do you know how many millions of dollars are spent on diet books a year? Do you know how many millions of dollars are spent on doctors, on buying pills or shots from the unborn calf of a baby elephant on the west coast of Mesapotamia, on eating scrambled eggs and tomatoes for three months, on drinking predigested protein without even asking who predigested it? Do you know why we put out those millions of dollars? I have a friend who's lost 900 pounds on those diets: loses 50, gains 80, loses 40, gains 20, loses 100, gains 120. You see, the fact is, every one of those diets probably works, but the day will arrive when you have to go off them. Now, if you understand the concept that you will be on a diet for the rest of your life, it is obvious immediately that none of those diets is going to work.

So now what we are going to do, instead of spending the million dollars, is to use common sense. Now, we are dealing with what I call normal weight problems; we are not dealing with extreme medical problems (and don't throw that line at me, "it's still baby fat," because I used it for thirty years; I don't want to hear about a nonmedical diagnosis of a thyroid condition, I used that one for ten or twelve years). What we are going to do is merely deal in common sense. Is there anyone who does not know cherry pie is fattening? A chocolate malt? See how smart you are? You're all diet experts. Common sense. You see, the fact is that if you don't think very highly of yourself, if behind here in this little niche in your head you know you're a dummy, because you never do anything right, why should you trust your common sense? Why should you trust your feelings, which are probably more accurate than anyone else's? So, you go out and spend all this money on diets, instead of knowing instinctively to keep your mouth shut, not to eat so much; instead of knowing what to eat and when to eat it; instead of knowing that exercise is important, because when you lose the weight, where do you think the skin goes?

I have gone into a dress shop and said, "I am going to a dinner party on Friday night. It's really important and I want something very special." "Oh, absolutely." They bring these five outfits in, and you try them on and you look. "What do you think?" "What do you think?" "Oh, Miss Bergen, that dress was maaaaaade for you." "You really think so?" Okay, so you buy the dress, and now this woman has just sold you a dress, right? She does not know whether you are going to wear this dress in a limousine, or a motorcycle, getting out of a Volkswagen, or in a plane. Do you live on a farm? Do you have to wade through seventeen inches of mud to get to the car? Do you have a penthouse? What is your lifestyle? How often will you wear that dress? Can you *sit* in it? (Do you know how many dresses I know that only stand? They only stand—skirts and pants that only stand. And when you sit, then stand, they sit.) You allowed that woman to sell you an outfit; that woman is paid to sell clothes. Are you going to tell me that you don't have as much sense of what looks good on you as anyone else? I know a thousand magazines out there that will give you an idea for a dress. I was born on a kitchen table in Bluegrass, Tennessee; I didn't live next door to a top model or Betty Grable or Eva Gabor or Cheryl Tiegs or any of those people. I didn't know. You read, you look, you buy, you learn, you educate yourself, and you trust your education. You use your common sense, you become responsible for your choice. "Oh, this dumb lady sold me this outfit at this store; well, she didn't tell me you couldn't sit in it." How could I have known? I could have sat in it.

And one by one, as you go down this list, you will make those changes that are important to you. Or you won't. A lot of people won't because, you see, it is easier not to make the change, it is easier to be what you are and use it as an excuse not to succeed. "Well, I can't help it, it's not my fault. I didn't get the job because I was too heavy," or "I didn't get the job because I was too thin, or I was too short, or I was too tall, or I had freckles, or I was black, I was yellow, I was green. My hair was too long, it was too curly, or it was *his* fault." It was *his* setting those rules that had nothing to do with *me*. So a lot of people won't be honest about what's important to them, because they don't want to compete.

Well, I'm telling you women that there are very few jobs for us at the top and you are going to have to get your priorities straight, with no excuses and no alibis. You'd better be responsible for what you're doing, and you'd better be willing to work seventy and eighty hours a week if you want to make it—if that's what you really want. If you want to take that responsibility, then you'd better be ready to do it. And don't think for one minute you can have a family and do it. You can have a family and work, but you can't have a family and get there. Know it now, I'm telling you now, you can't. Now's the time for you to know it—you can't. It's too bad you can't, maybe, but you can't. Because up there is more work than you can possibly imagine, because we have to work, unfortunately, right now, twice as hard as any guy to get there. And even then, we may not get there—because 80 percent of the jobs today for women are clerical, sales, menial, secretarial. Women with college degrees earn 40 percent less than men with high school degrees. So decide—because you're going to have to work really hard and you're going to have to know what your priorities are. Well, the fact is that 90 percent of you in your lifetime are going to have to work, whether *you* want to or not. In most families today, husbands and wives both work—that's the only way they can keep up. They're the only ones who are getting mortgages on their houses, they're the only ones who are buying cars, they're the only ones who are taking vacations, they're the only ones who are buying the big-unit pieces: microwave ovens, refrigerators, televisions, and stereos. You'd better be prepared to take the responsibility for yourself. You'd better be prepared also to use common sense. You'd better know yourself: you'd better know your limitations, and you'd better know the scope of your possibilities.

I have a very simple saying—I don't know whether it's true for everybody, but I know it works for me—I always believed I could be anything in the world I wanted to be. Now, obviously, you can't be an opera singer if you can't carry a tune, so we're not talking about wild schemes. We're talking about reality. If you want to work hard enough for it, not dream about it, hope it will happen, you have to work for it. Maybe you don't want to work that hard, and that's okay. Maybe you don't want to work at all; I hope you don't have to. Maybe you'll work a little and have a family, too, and that's super and wonderful and fulfilling and terrific. All those different situations can be fulfilling and wonderful and terrific, but know what each one of them requires of you; know who you are inside. Don't discover it when you're forty-one and scared out of your wits; discover it now. Know now how you feel about you and deal with it now.

When you've finally gone through everything on the left side of the list, you can move to the right side of the list: things you like about you. You know how to use those things, to make them work for you, to make you the special person you are. A few of you may think, "That's terrific"; that's easy for you to think. But on that side of my sheet I haven't written anything. My eyes are too small and too close together, I have a funny nose, my hair is silly, and my body is funny. There's a woman I know in New York; I'd say she's in her early thirties, maybe. She has small beady eyes and a very funny, large, awkward nose and a very angular sort of face; her hair is dyed absolutely coal black (which, I hope, most of us realize is not a natural color); she has this very white skin; and she wears brilliant red lipstick. And she is usually very stylishly dressed. She has a very simple, elegant way of dressing. She's a beautiful dresser. Not high fashion—she wears a lot of black, and she always wears something red, a red flower or red belt or red scarf. She has great style, but she is horsefaced. I'm getting into this only because I don't want you to think we're talking just about physical beauty; that is meaningless. This woman will walk into a party where every gorgeous woman and man in New York City may be, as well as every bright and intelligent mind. And within fifteen minutes she will have wrapped up the entire room; they will all be crowded around her, listening to what she has to say and being involved in a conversation, a communication with her, because what she has on the right side of her page is her love and concern for, her interest in the people around her. You can't tell her enough about yourself, she's interested in everything; she absorbs information, she is fascinated by your life—I don't care whether you're a farmer or a nuclear scientist. Do you know how hard it is to dislike someone who's crazy about you; who thinks you're intelligent, who hangs on every word? She's not phony (even I spot phony); she really does care. You see, she put it all together: she took who she was, as each one of us can do because each one of us is special, and she made that work for her. And she is special, not a poor imitation of someone else, not copying so-and-so's hairdo and somebody else's makeup, a lousy imitation of an original. All of you are originals. She is an original, and spectacular.

Barbra Streisand is an original. There are children who are growing and will never get their noses fixed because Barbra Streisand made that nose okay. She evaluated who she was, and she decided what worked for her and what didn't. As she grew up and became more secure, those things started to come together until she is who she is, an individual, a special person. You may like her, you may not like her, but she is who she is. She does not play games, she does not seek "yes votes," she is responsible for herself, she is a partner and can be a partner to anyone. Would you not rather have a partner in life than either someone who is your boss or someone whom you boss? Look toward the partner.

And you get through the list. It's a silly, funny list; it's a purely physical list, but funny how, as you deal with each little thing— short, stumpy legs or an age—you see inside yourself. You see an attitude about those things.

Well, it took me a few years, and I've still got a lot of years to go, probably, before I really get it all together. But I do know one thing. I know that I spent forty-nine years pretending to be beautiful, pretending to be intelligent, pretending to be sexy, pretending to be a warm and loving friend. And now I finally know that I really am beautiful, and I really am intelligent, and I really am sexy, and I really am a warm and loving friend. I have learned and will continue to learn how to manage and please the top manager—*me*.

TWO

Personal Economics
for Today's Woman

Sylvia Auerbach

Sylvia Auerbach developed and taught a course entitled "Women and Money" at the New School for Social Research, at Barnard College, and at New York University. She has authored A Woman's Book of Money *and* Your Money: How to Make it Stretch. *A frequent guest and panelist on radio and television, she has also lectured around the United States to audiences interested in more effective ways to direct their financial future.*

I want to give you some food for thought, and what better setting than to envision yourself at a dinner party. Wait for one of those inevitable lulls in the conversation and just lean across the table and say to your host or hostess, in a voice loud enough to be heard by the assemblage, "By the way, how much do you earn?" Can you imagine the shocked silence that would follow? (You would probably never get invited again!) Well-bred, polite

15

people do *not* talk about money in public, and do not ask about incomes. It would be far less shocking if you asked someone, "How's your sex life?"

Why is this? When we talk of money, we're not talking about coins and currency—we are talking about the things that money represents to each of us. While the psychological and Freudian aspects of money are fascinating, I want to examine one aspect of money that all of us comprehend and that men throughout the ages have understood and used. Money is *power*.

People without money are powerless; people who control money have some control over the lives of others. People who dispense money are independent; people who must defer to or rely on others for money are dependents. These basic facts have, in the past, defined where women stood. And until women understand the power of money, control some money, are willing to manage money, and above all *have equal opportunities to earn incomes comparable to men's,* they will always play a dependent role.

I would love to say that when I talk about dependency and inequality I am reminiscing—how things were in the bad old days. That's just not true, and I'm going to show you with facts and figures. Women are still patronized and condescended to by some bankers, accountants, lawyers, colleagues, and men they meet socially. At dinner parties I am still getting the same reactions I got when I first wrote my book *A Woman's Book of Money.* Husbands accuse me of being a "troublemaker"; wives—very often professional women—say, "I don't know why it is but when people begin to talk about money I can feel my eyes getting glazed, or I get turned off, or I think yes, yes—but I'll do it later."

Why is this? Something in our genes, chromosomes? Not at all—it's the way we have been socialized. We've been raised to think of ourselves as mothers, nurturers, and helpmates—all honorable roles certainly, but dependent ones. And we have filled these roles in the business world as well as at home; on the fringes of power rather than at the center. Let me review just briefly what I call the garbage vs. guile scene.

Children see early where power lies, with the person who has the most money, still usually the man. Girls are taught to wheedle for their allowance; little boys are expected to put out the garbage for theirs. Little girls are so enchanting that fathers indulge them—and they grow up not believing or accepting the fact that managing money is one of their adult responsibilities. Boys are told that some day they will be providers, money is something for which they have to be responsible. Girls are encouraged to be bargain hunters; boys are encouraged to take risks.

This same kind of learning pattern is reinforced by the jobs women have held—the lower level, middle management jobs that didn't involve financial planning. Accompanying this lack of financial control and management experience is a feeling of inferiority—a lack of confidence and self-esteem, a denigration of women's abilities in the business world and at home. Remember that the chores women do at home have no measurable monetary value in the economy, and are not even considered in the gross national product. There is an interaction between the fact that economists and the world in general put such a low value on women's work at home and the fact that women themselves do, too.

One result of this undervaluation is the burden that women bear, no matter what their individual choices as to lifestyle. In the not-so-distant past women who worked outside their homes were considered freaks, neurotics, somehow not quite feminine, bad mothers, threatening wives. And so of course they felt guilty, even when they were working, as more and more of them were, for such "pin money" items as the mortgage; college tuition; a replacement for the about-to-die family car, or washing machine, or refrigerator.

Now the picture has changed drastically, and women who *don't* work are made to feel guilty. Why aren't they out there contributing to the family income—being super-moms; managing not only to hold down jobs, but also to have careers? It's a no-win situation, in a world which theoretically, at least, has just about achieved equality.

But—and it is a very big *but*—some of us are still more equal than others. The essence of personal economics is planning, but I maintain that men and women plan their personal economics in a different environment. I'm going to defend my viewpoint by discussing five different areas in which women are still at a disadvantage. First: the salary gap. Figures just issued by the Women's Bureau of the U.S. Department of Labor based on the latest data (1977) indicate that "women have to work nearly nine days to earn as much as men earn in five days; men working *full time* had a median income of $14,626 while women earned only $8,618." Put another way, women earned only 59 cents for every dollar that men earned.

More dismal figures: where do women work to achieve (!!!) their disparate earnings. You know and I know that they are—80 percent of them—in the clerical, sales, service, and plant or factory jobs. The remaining 20 percent are concentrated in the professions, but often with different jobs or job titles than men, and, needless to say, different salaries. Though this is changing, men are still the dominant sex as doctors, lawyers, college professors with tenure, and presidents of large corporations and banks. Women are the nurses, lawyers who are not partners, assistant professors, instructors without tenure, and middle managers. Since I was once managing editor of the *Library Journal,* I thought I'd check and see how things are in that career area. I quote from an article in the 15 December 1979 *Library Journal,* titled "Sexism in the Library Profession": "out of 80 major public libraries in the United States, 71 are headed by men and only 9 are headed by women."

In the general labor market one important new development is the decision by the AFL-CIO, at its recent convention, to support the concept of "equal pay for comparable work." This could considerably reduce the wage and income disparities that make women second-class citizens economically.

It is a movement that got its impetus from the Coalition of Labor Union Women, who have been pressing their cause for years, but this is the first time that labor has considered backing this demand. The International Union of Electrical Workers now has a suit pending against Westinghouse in Trenton, New Jersey; their suit argues that women are paid less than men in jobs requiring equivalent skills.

This is a complex problem, especially once you get beyond the routine tasks—usually in factories—that can be measured fairly easily. Nevertheless, as women we must pay attention to it, since the informal designation of an occupation as "women's work" has in the past always meant "lower paid work." Again it is a *societal issue,* because men, too, will benefit if a pool of lower-cost labor is eliminated from the marketplace. And union leaders are well aware that the great untapped potential reservoir for new members is the service field—in which women predominate.

But how about those who have made it? Where do they stand? Have they really "made it"? Heidrick and Struggles, a management consulting firm, did a profile of the woman officer in the 1,300 largest U.S. companies in 1978. Here's what they found: Fewer than one in four are vice-presidents or higher; in fact 55.5 percent were at the corporate secretary or assistant corporate secretary rank. "Not a single one of the dozen perquisites offered to men were given to the majority of women officers," though most men had accepted them.

What are these "perks"? Company cars, sometimes with chauffeurs; super offices; extra-long vacations; and memberships in hunting clubs, fishing clubs, or just private lunch clubs. Remember, these clubs are not just social—they are places where important deals are transacted. Heidrick and Struggles went on to say that "only three 'perks,' stock options, medical examinations and extra life insurance, are held by a preponderance even of those women making $40,000 or more." And according to the U.S. Department of Commerce, only 392,442 women earned $25,000 or more in 1977, the most recent figure available.

Now let's look at some of the reasons women don't earn more. I wouldn't, in fact couldn't, begin to duplicate the work done in *The Managerial Woman,* that excellent book by Anne Jardim and Margaret Hennig. But let me point out some more prosaic reasons that hold women back from the executive suite on the fortieth floor. A 1979 study of working mothers (i.e., *women employed outside their homes,* a definition I prefer, since all mothers with young children are working mothers) showed that while 92 percent said their husbands shared in the care of the children, 85 percent said the traditional housekeeping chores—shopping, cooking, and cleaning—are still their responsibility. This has also been documented in other studies of the two-paycheck family. Caroline Bird, in her excellent book, *The Two-Paycheck Marriage,* says, "Wives contribute 40 percent of the earnings of working couples, but every trick known to accountants is used to ensure that their money doesn't count as much as his." (And of course, if she earns less, as she probably does, she doesn't feel she has equal clout.)

Ah, well, say employers, *women are out more than men because they're sick.* The fact is that for childless men and women the absentee rates are the same. But surveys have shown that women report themselves "sick" when actually they are home taking care of sick children, or taking children to the doctor or dentist. Since companies don't pay for sick leave if it's a child who is sick, and women can't afford to lose part of their already smaller paycheck, they say *they* are sick.

Now let's talk about the divorced woman—who has also been called the "new poor." If she's been out of the job market for a while and then goes back in, you know and I know that she starts at a lower level and probably never makes up the years she was at home with a child. Furthermore, when decisions are made on child support, no dollar figure is put on the value of her child care—in line with the fact that no dollar figure has been put on it even when she was a wife. To add injury to insult, repeated surveys have said that child support payments fail to provide for even half of the children in divorced families, which is topped by the fact that the vast majority of fathers don't keep up their support payments—even when they can easily afford them. (The size of this problem isn't known precisely, partly because it's so expensive and troublesome for women to collect that they just don't bother.)

Incidentally, no-fault divorce laws have been blamed by lawyers and sociologists for a decline in child support. No-fault relieved fathers of responsibilities and took away one of the few weapons that women had. Karen Seal, an instructor at Grossmon College, California, studied 600 California divorce cases and found that child support *dropped* from an average of $75 a month in 1968 to an average of $61 in 1976.

This is such a tale of gloom and doom that I'd like to digress and repeat a few of my favorite money quotations. Here is one from Oscar Wilde:

"Let us all be happy and live within our means, even if we have to borrow to do it."

Another: "If money go before, all ways do lie open" (Shakespeare).

Finally: "So long as he is rich, even a barbarian is attractive" (Ovid).

Of course, I've told you the worst side, because I think coping starts with being realistic about the environment we're in and the roles we play. Now I'd like to stress that we have all come a long way. There are women in every field and profession, and in their own businesses. Salary discrimination is waning, and opportunities are increasing. Money is more equally shared in marriage, and more women realize that money is their province as much as a man's—that they not only understand it but can manage it well. Handling money is not a sex-related function; it is something that some of us do superbly, male or female; some of us do badly, male or female; and most of us are somewhere in the middle.

Now I'd like to describe how to improve your skills in managing money. I wish I could offer you a perfect plan—something like the perfect diet, where you eat all you want of your favorite, and of course fattening, foods and still get thin. We all know there is no such diet; and there is also no foolproof, guaranteed-to-succeed money plan that will allow you to spend all you want, as you please, and still come out solvent. I can, however, suggest some practical, realistic guidelines that I believe will help you become a better money manager. They are based on my research, experience, teaching, consulting work—and mistakes!

What is your goal? It is to become a money *manager*, not a money spender. And your aim is also to balance your personal priorities with your resources. Your money is the means for achieving the lifestyle you want. What are your tools? Very simple. Some sharpened pencils, a big tablet, your most recent tax return, a ruler—and a mirror. Take a look in that mirror and ask yourself a personal question: what's your financial personality type? Does the word *budget* set up an instant, completely negative reaction? Do you feel it is absolutely beyond your capabilities to budget, and you know from experience it doesn't pay to try. In fact, does the word *budget* make you so uneasy that you sometimes, almost defiantly, go out and buy something extravagant—as if to prove that you can't do it?

Or do you go to the other extreme and pinch every penny, denying yourself things that you really can afford—worrying that thirty years from now you might be poverty-stricken? Neither attitude is sensible, or necessary. And both allow money to assume too important a place in your daily life. Your first task is to decide what you value that money buys. It's important to know, because it affects your spending patterns and habits and your potential for successful money management. You need to plan your finances in a very personal way—to fit you as it would fit no other individual—or the plan won't work.

Does this attitude make you feel guilty? Do you feel that it's somehow or other not "right" to consider your personality, the time you have available, and your lifestyle when deciding how to handle money. If so, get some reassurance from no less an authority than Dr. Herbert Simon, the 1978 winner of the Nobel prize in economics. Dr. Simon's award was based on his research on how managers make business decisions. Everyone assumed that managers fed data into computers, knew all costs from five years' worth of oil to the going price for old pencil stubs, and then made completely rational decisions based on carefully researched alternatives.

False. It turns out from Dr. Simon's research that managers are not and cannot be all that thorough, well-informed, careful, and rational. They can only guess at what oil prices will be in five years—and they have a bad record on guesses. They may like to take the pencil stubs home for the kiddies to play with. They're not sure who is the best supplier for Brand X and don't have the time to spend finding out. It may pay them to give the Product X order to their old college classmate and golf companion, with the well-justified expectation that he will reciprocate, in due time, with a big order for their company's Product Y.

In other words, *according to Dr. Simon, decision-making is costly in time and resources and complete information is hard to come by. So man-*

agers select reasonable and possible solutions, given the circumstances they work under. They *"satisfice" (the word he uses),* i.e., *they choose acceptable solutions to problems.* That's what I'm suggesting to you. You, too, can win a prize, better money management in these unsettling times, by satisficing. You simply don't have the time to learn *all* the possible alternatives; to get the most recent information on prices, rates of interest, and best buys; or to analyze accurately the probability of certain things happening in the future.

Does this mean that you just go along in the same old way? No, it doesn't. When I asked Dr. Simon what he would advise someone who is not getting along and not managing her money well, he said the first question to ask would be "Why?" Would you really find a change in your lifestyle to one that was more affordable that dissatisfying? Would you really be that unhappy if you changed? A good question to ponder, this may be just the impetus you need to get out of that "But-I've-always-done-it-this-way, bought-this, worn-that, can't-get-along-without rut." Satisficing doesn't mean never making changes. You need to spend as much time and energy as you can in solving your money problems, making the best possible decisions with the information and resources available. Then you can stop worrying and get on with the business of living. And now for some help in making decisions.

Where to start? With a basic strategy, a win-the-money-game plan. This is the time to make every penny stand up and be counted. You need a financial plan, and here is one tried and true way to go about getting one.

Step One: Write down your total annual income, counting only income that you're sure of. Forget bonuses and commissions, unless they're guaranteed. Deduct from this figure total federal, state, and local taxes, so you can see your real take-home pay.

Step Two: Write down all the annual expenses that this income must cover. These expenses should be divided into two categories, fixed and variable. *Fixed (or contractual) expenses* are those that can't be changed easily with the one-year period we're discussing, e.g., rent. *Variable expenses* are those over which you have some control (though it may be limited) such as clothing and household expenses. Consult such records as your tax return and check book to get an accurate idea of what these expenses are.

Step Three: Decide how much you need for an emergency fund. How long could you survive if you lost your job and had to live on your savings and unemployment compensation? What would you do if your car finally gave up the ghost? What would you live on if you were seriously sick for several months? Decide on an amount you are comfortable with and plan to make regular deposits into this emergency fund until you have the fund that you need. To be sure you have such an emergency fund, consider deposits into it as a *fixed expense* that can't be skipped. Go back to step two and add it on to fixed expenses.

Step Four: Add the fixed and variable expenses and deduct this figure from your "real income." The balance that remains is often called "discretionary income," i.e., money that can be used for purposes outside of, or in addition to, day-to-day living expenses (even some that are indiscreet!).

Hopefully your real take-home income exceeds your fixed and variable expenses. You are now in a position to examine your discretionary income, deciding what you can and cannot afford, setting up a list of priorities and/or objectives, and planning how to achieve them.

What if you find that your discretionary income doesn't allow for these objectives, or not in the way that you would like? What then? You have several alternatives, not all of which are going to make you clap your hands and jump for joy. You may have to rearrange your ideas somewhat or give up some idea altogether. For instance: Your objective is a month's deluxe vacation in Europe this year. Your plan shows you can't afford it. You scale that down to two weeks in Europe staying at low-cost pensiones, or you postpone the trip until next year, or you decide to go to the local beach for two weeks.

You might find that you have to make even more drastic changes: start brown-bagging your lunch; forget new clothes for this year; or give up your weekly exercise class.

The choices are up to you—and they have to be right or wrong for you, though they might be exactly opposite from

choices your best friend would make. If they depress you, remember that they're not immutable—they are decisions that you
are making now so that your finances are under your control:
they can always be changed and improved as you get ahead in
your career.

Step Five: Set up a system and time frame for implementing
your decisions. So far you've been dealing with annual figures;
now you can break these down into the most convenient time
period. You'll probably want this period to mesh with your
paycheck, but a month is usually the most convenient way to do
it. Let's say you decide on a month-by-month period. You start
by setting aside enough, every month, to cover each of your
monthly fixed and variable expenses. Next, you deposit a specific
amount each month to cover those expenses that don't occur
monthly but have to be worked into the budget, for instance,
semiannual tuition payments or insurance premiums.

You follow the same procedure in setting aside the funds
needed for your lifestyle objectives, e.g., that European vacation.
If you think you "can't save," have a specified sum automatically
taken out of your salary by your employer or your bank and
deposited in a savings account. Finally, you set up some kind of
calendar to remind you when certain infrequent payments are
due.

Step Six: Deposit any money not needed for ongoing expenses
into some kind of interest-bearing account, the more the juicier,
depending on what's available by way of such accounts, and how
much money you have to set aside.

Step Seven: Plan for a regular review to see how close you've
come to your target in alloting your funds and how well the
budget works. In the beginning, you might want to make a quar-
terly check, and you'll probably have to make some changes.
(Who can predict in advance what will happen to the price of
lettuce?) But after some initial adding here and subtracting there
you should be able to stay comfortably within your guidelines
and settle for a year-end review.

And some more comments by Dr. Simon. It's important for all
of us periodically to review our routines and priorities. We always need a sensible pattern to guide our actions. He quotes Mr.

Micawber in *David Copperfield:* "Annual income, twenty pounds, annual expenditure, nineteen six, result happiness. Annual income twenty pounds, annual expenditure, twenty pounds ought and six, result misery."

Now, let me mention briefly what happens in many two-career families. Good salaries, both partners. Good earnings prospects. So what would you expect—a nice fat bankroll, some money put aside, and a good standard of living, right? Alas, two-thirds wrong. The good standard of living, yes—but no bankroll, and virtually no savings. In fact, such couples are frequently in debt beyond their incomes. Why? Overoptimism, and an unrealistic appraisal of their spending limits. There seems to be so much money that they never bother to plan, and consequently get into debt. Just a word of warning.

And a follow-up word of warning. When the female half of this couple leaves her job to have a baby, she sometimes finds herself—since she hasn't been part of planned financial teamwork—getting more and more ignorant about family finances. She abdicates, because she is truly very, very busy. If the marriage is a good one, she nevertheless finds herself feeling guilty about spending money on herself; somehow or other what had been "their money" becomes "his money" and she reverts to a "dependent" state of mind and actions. This new mind-set often makes her resentful, makes her husband feel overburdened, and is an unfortunate role model for her daughters and her sons.

This isn't healthy, but what's even worse is the situation if the marriage breaks up. I have met these women in my classes and heard their really sad stories of being cheated out of their fair share of the property and other assets because they had lost track of what they owned. You have the responsibility to yourself to keep informed about your finances, to know what insurance policies you and/or your spouse have, what assets you have, and whose name or names are on the title, to *have* a will, and to know what's in your husband's will. End of lecture.

You also owe it to yourself to be an investor by making a big investment in your own future. I am frequently asked what can be done about inflation, and I think one of the best answers is to invest in your own training so that you realize all your potential, and therefore your ability to earn more. And the more productive we all are, the more we have to contribute to the society we live in.

Now, having discussed what you as an individual can do, I want to emphasize that you cannot, *should not,* have to do it alone. The economic issues we face as women, so basic to everything else we do, are not our issues but society's issues. And they should always be viewed from a societal viewpoint, if we are to have not "liberated women" but "liberated human beings."

Briefly let's examine the woman in what is described accurately as the typical American family today. It is comprised of a husband who has a full-time job and a wife who has a full or part-time job; about half of these families have children under eighteen. (Statistics in this field come from a variety of sources—Women's Bureau, Bureau of Labor Statistics, Department of Commerce—and they are somewhat fuzzy, depending on how the terms are defined.) A family with two children in their teens has a different problem than a family with two children under six. Nevertheless, the point I want to make is that the current American Dream, the individual suburban house with limited or almost nonexistent public transportation, is a difficult arrangement for the employed family with children, and particularly the mother who typically has two jobs—her outside job and her job as household manager.

She needs time and services, and the suburbs almost conspire to use too much of her time and make services too hard to get. She cannot afford the time it takes to commute to the higher-paying jobs usually found in the city; nor can she rely on her husband, who has a long commute. It is difficult to find domestic helpers, since they cannot get to her without transportation. Teenagers also have a hard time getting around.

I believe that one of the major problems facing us is to evolve housing that is planned with employed families in mind: public transportation (a greater necessity now that oil is scarce) and a community combination nursery school, regular school, and after-school center. Such a center could utilize the pool of teachers now facing unemployment. These professionals could easily be retrained to be part of all-day child care programs. Centers could use the talents of local teenagers to help care for the younger children while better preparing them for family life; they could also draw on the talents of senior citizens who have much to contribute—especially to single-parent families.

We have to continue the trend toward flex-time jobs, for *men* and for women. This is a trend that is growing, not out of altruism but because employers recognize that they are the ones who benefit. The December 1979 *CPA Client Bulletin,* published by the American Institute of Certified Public Accountants, had this comment: "having trouble finding someone to fill a *key* position: why not look for two people to fill it? . . . Employers who adopt job-sharing do so because, although it increases employment-related paperwork and causes other inconveniences, it brings aboard people whose *skills* would not otherwise be available [my italics]."

Another possibility is taking advantage of new technology to allow more work to be done at home. Women in publishing already work at home with *old* technology, namely editing pencils, typewriters, and *brains.* But the Continental Illinois National Bank and Trust Company in Chicago has a word-processing department partially staffed by women who work at home using a terminal on line with the bank's main office.

I want to make a strong point here that women who work at home must have *supporting* services—just as much as the mother who works elsewhere. The woman at home needs child care, help with her housework, the possibility of buying prepared foods and—dream of dreams—having them delivered.

In some ways apartment houses in major metropolitan areas have already adapted to the world of the employed, with their desks for receiving packages, in-house cleaning services, and shoe repair and dry-cleaning shops. Why can't they also be planned with in-house restaurants, cafeteria-style or cafeteria-style-plus (at a price) service, so that good meals are available in a family setting—from breakfast to after-school snacks to dinner?

And why not apartment houses built or converted to have space set aside for a nursery and after-school center? I believe such buildings would be profitable and, in fact, would have waiting lists of tenants, but in the beginning there could, if needed, be tax advantages to builders who put up such buildings.

That brings up another question of importance to women's economic well-being: our tax laws. We must press for a higher child-care allowance. The maximum credit of $400 for one dependent or $800 for two or more is completely out of date in today's economy. I can tell you, from personal knowledge, that it isn't even one month's tax-deductible rent on apartments that corporations maintain in New York City for occasional use by their executives for various kinds of socializing and entertainment.

Why am I convinced that this is society's problem, not women's? Because I have shared in the anguish of young couples, particularly the mothers, of course, as they searched desperately for someone reliable to look after their young children. Sometimes the only answer has been for the mother to drop out of the labor market for a while—which means she really never catches up on her career and society is deprived of the use of her education and skills.

Or, because of the trauma, I know other young couples who decide against having children—so that the best educated and most highly trained portion of our population is the group that is not reproducing itself. That is society's loss, and theirs—because I believe, speaking as a mother, that having children is one of life's joys.

Women count. We have a very important role to play in our economic environment. Since we are the major purchasing agents in the consumer sector of the economy, we can vote with our dollars for companies that promote women fairly and equally; that make safe products; that advertise responsibly; that offer help to working mothers, such as flex-time and child care.

We are already making a tremendous contribution to our society, on the job and at home, and our roles will continue to grow and expand.

Now let me end on a very personal note about money. So often in my classes women say, "This is probably a very stupid question, but. . . ." If you don't know the answer, no question is stupid. The only really stupid thing is not to know—and not to ask. It could be a very expensive mistake, and one which macho men have often made. Remember that all experts at some time slip into the jargon of their trade. (And some not-so-experts slip into the jargon in the hopes that you won't ask them!) Never be bashful about asking if you don't understand something.

And remember that the *real expert in your personal economic plan* is yourself. You are the only one who knows your own purse and priorities. It's your life—and your money. I wish you the best of luck in spending both enjoyably.

THREE

Communicating

and Managing

the Media Challenge

Lenore Hershey

Lenore Hershey is currently editor of the Ladies' Home Journal, *a position she has held since 1973. She is also vice-president of Ladies' Home Journal Publishing, Inc.*

She was a member of the President's National Commission for the Observance of International Women's Year and a member of the Presidential Advisory Committee on the Economic Role of Women.

Ms. Hershey received an honorary Doctor of Letters from Marymount College in 1977. She was named one of the twenty-five most influential women in America. In 1973 she was honored by the New York City National Council of Christians and Jews as one of fifty extraordinary women of achievements and has been cited as Mother of the Year by the Talbot Perkins Children's Services.

My vocation as a magazine editor is essentially one of artist and craftsman; I tend to trust my imagination and judgment more than I do a computer. My criteria are largely inherited from the world of journalism, where money may be the unseen sinew but where service and truth must remain the soul. Yet, as an executive, I am painfully aware of Damon Runyon's law, which grows more pertinent with every passing year. The Runyon rule: "The race is not always to the swift, nor the battle to the strong, but that's the way to bet."

So, with full awareness of the odds, I will attempt to impart to you that media people—and especially women media people— can no longer afford to live in ivory towers.

While my references will be mostly about magazines, the same forces are operating in television, radio, newspapers, advertising, and public relations. Most of us who hold jobs in these fields are probably there because of an ego-drive that told us we had special talents in those directions. Possibly, too, we were under the impression that these areas had an aura of power, glamour, and social prestige. Upon occasion they still do. But those of us who by choice or chance have moved closer to the top know that the message is not in the headline, but in the bottom line. You don't have a secure job if your company is not making a profit. You have a rosier future if you are helping your company to make more money. It is better to be on the side of the swift and the strong than to run with the losers. Those are the fact of life, as grubby as they sound. If you wish to be an executive in the private sector, you had better learn to live with them.

I started as a writer, which I still am. But a long series of opportunities and experience turned me into the editor-in-chief of *Ladies' Home Journal,* a great women's magazine that's been around for almost a century. I am almost seven years into the job, and I still find it mostly rewarding fun, if I can be allowed that nonmanagerial expression. I have also grown fiscally sophisticated. One tends to lose one's economic virginity when one handles a multi-million-dollar budget and attends frequent financial planning meetings at which everyone is using a pocket computer—everyone except me. I prefer to "look at the long-range overview."

That is what I'll do now—because magazines, and indeed all media, today are facing new and increased economic pressures, technical demands, and tough earnings mandates from the financial corporations which now largely control them. If editors aren't aware of the forces shaping their destinies, their destinies can slip away from them. It is a difficult lesson to pass on to some of my younger editors, who see financial facts as a threat to their editorial integrity, or perhaps who have math weakness in their scholastic backgrounds. So do I. But when I took a three-day Wharton course in financial management a few years ago, I not only kept afloat, but learned to read a balance sheet, and feel a lot more confident for it.

Why does an editor today have to be a competent manager in a great many aspects of his or her job? Because even though an editor must put out and orchestrate a product that requires literary, artistic, and social judgments, editing today is also a matter of marketing. *Ladies' Home Journal* today is a magazine with a circulation of 5,500,000 copies—about fourteen million readers. *Ladies' Home Journal* readers are a marketing entity because the magazine is a definitive personality. Through both our packaging and our content we are saying to millions of women every month: *We are here to inform, to amuse, to help, to bolster, to give you your money's worth and a little more. We know your needs and your tastes. We have somehow put together this month a mixture to stimulate you, satisfy you, and perhaps even surprise you.*

Some of this can be done with gut-feeling and experience. But much of it has to stem from informed management. That's where communications comes in. We have some available currents of research, which tell us what and where our reader is and how she's living. For example, we know that half our *Journal* readership today works either part or full time outside the home, which is an important factor in the planning of our editorial. We know that our median age is somewhere in the high thirties, although the recent answers—30,000 of them—to a *Journal* marriage questionnaire revealed a median age of about 32. Our various service editors keep in touch with the food, fashion, beauty, and home decorating needs of our audience through mail and personal contact. We all follow marketing trends in every area, and watch carefully to see which celebrities and personalities are swimming into public favor—or at least into public attention.

Yes, a magazine editor does not flinch at that word *saleable*. A magazine must have a function, and it must be saleable—both on subscription and at the newsstand, which is more and more the supermarket rack. Indeed, the old term *circulation department* has given way to *consumer marketing,* and perhaps it's a good thing because it reminds me and my staff that we are not in this business to amuse ourselves but to please consumers and to satisfy a need for readers—at a price they're willing to pay, even in tough times.

But there is another *m* besides *marketing*—*management*—which looms large. As I said, I operate a large budget, and am compelled by my upper management to stay within it. To do that, I must keep track of all my operating costs, from the overhead to salaries to the price of engravings to the money paid for manuscripts, properties, photographers, and art.

According to the Magazine Publishers Association, editorial costs on magazines, always a low percentage of the total cost of putting out a magazine, have actually gone down from 10 percent to 6 percent. I suspect this is largely because everything else has proportionately skyrocketed: paper, production, mailing, distribution. However, it is also due to more prudent editorial buying, and the fact that there aren't too many major properties out there for magazines. *Princess Daisy,* for example, was totally impossible to cut for magazine use; and its author, Judy Krantz, who used to write for the *Journal,* finally withdrew it from magazine rights entirely. When a winner does come along, competition grows fierce, and all of us editors sit like poker players in our own offices trying to outbid each other.

I am not alone in my financial management responsibilities. I work with a publisher whose total responsibility is the business of the magazine, and we both report to an executive vice-president who is a financial whiz and who gives me all my management rhetoric about optimizing my growth opportunities and increasing earnings performance. I also work with our circulation director—I mean, our consumer marketing expert—who is now responsible for almost half the money that keeps the *Journal* on the profit side. And I am not above being cordial, friendly, and informative to the advertising department, which accounts for the other half of the incoming dollars.

Journalism students still have the misconception that magazines are full of pages that plug products to please advertisers. This simply is not true. Ralph Nader has written for us for years, and he has never done a column saying, for example, that all cosmetics age women. If he did, and if he could prove it, which even Ralph Nader can't do, I don't think I'd have any hesitation about running the item. On the other hand, it is equally true that an editor can talk to advertising sales people—and indeed to advertisers and their agencies—without losing their integrity. We are marketing to women; so are they. Often we can learn from each other.

Our advertising sales people, and a growing proportion of them are women, do not spend their days in our editors' offices. But they are entitled to hear from me, and from others on our staff, what we are trying to create and what our thrust is. Our circulation department, if they are to do their job well, must know far ahead what's coming up, who and what are being featured.

So must our promotion and publications departments. I don't think the ordinary public today realizes how much media must be backed by marketing in these competitive days. *People* magazine, with its phenomenal newsstand sales, is backed by a newspaper, radio, and TV advertising budget in excess of $8 million a year. Time-Life, which launched *People,* is one of the real pros at introducing and selling magazines; and they spend with a lavish hand that seems in almost every case to come back full of business and profits.

We don't have or spend that kind of money on the *Journal,* unfortunately, and must stand on our own ingenious methods. That is why recently I devoted a full morning to two of our regular preview meetings. One was for our advertising sales and publishing staff. John Stevens, our managing editor, and I went through the entire book, explaining why and how each story had been planned, telling some behind-the-scenes stories, and giving a summation of how this issue carries the *Journal* forward in its identity. John then went on to bring the same message to our Chicago staff. This meeting was followed by a pre-preview meeting, with rough galleys, the first proof of the cover, and a run-through of what we are going to have in a succeeding month. This was for the benefit of our circulation staff, which knows which cities to concentrate on for added sales; for our promotion people, who are planning trade and general promotion; and for our public relations aides. Last week I had my annual visit to Hollywood to present Star-Dazzle Awards on the "Merv Griffin Show." The awardees this year were Bo Derek, Sissy Spacek, Loni Anderson, Marsha Mason, and author Judith Krantz. I must admit that this yearly event is pretty heady stuff, and I love it. But so are our prestigious Women of the Year awards, also televised. These also represent hundreds of thousands of dollars of free TV time in which *Ladies' Home Journal* is promoted to millions of new readers.

I enjoy the opportunity to speak or to write about *Ladies' Home Journal.* The reason: an editor can somehow define the objectives and character of a magazine better than anyone else. I'm proud of what our staff has done recently to make the *Journal* a magazine for the contemporary woman, with all her changing tastes and demographics. I always smile sweetly when an intense young woman in an audience speaks about the *Journal* as if it had never given up bustles and dust-ruffles. The truth is that we are no longer the magazine your mother read. That's where management comes in. We must keep moving to accommodate new lifestyles, new attitudes, and new impacts on our readers' behavior. And we must project, not just for next month or next year, but for at least five years ahead. A magazine must always have its eye on the future, or it becomes a landmark of the past.

Editors-in-chief have had to learn about financial planning because so many of them are now parts of large corporations. *Ladies' Home Journal,* like its sister publication *Redbook,* is under the aegis of a company called Charter Media. The chairman and CEO will not interfere with editorial, but will hold it accountable to pull its full share in making profits for the company. It would be fun to edit a small magazine from a rolltop desk and keep your own books. But small operations are few and far apart, and one must learn to live with the systems that are an inevitable part of corporate life. Corporations today are awash with red tape, most of it made mandatory by government procedures.

My good friend, Geraldine Rhoads, who is editor-in-chief of *Woman's Day* magazine, recently acquired by CBS, told some interesting stories at a recent conference for editors sponsored by ASME, the American Society of Magazine Editors. For example, she can commit her book to hundreds of thousands of dollars of magazine properties, but she cannot replace an employee who resigns without getting a bunch of signatures on a paper. Her signature is also requisite, she says, for every subscription requisition. Expense accounts are also carefully checked, and lawsuits abound, largely because CBS seems such a good target.

We have had some lawsuits, but not many. Every article must be checked by our company lawyer; and our contracts with writers, photographers, and artists regularly grow more complicated. Lawyers, accountants, and human resources department heads (that used to be called personnel) are all part of my daily activities. Sometimes I seem to read more company memos than I do manuscripts. I should tell you, I do not favor the memorandum form. I'd rather pick up the phone or go to the office of the person involved. But corporations seem to get over their identity crises by memo.

Incidentally, in listing my contacts, I have seemingly left out one of the most important: manufacturing. By some gift of the gods, I don't have to supervise these budgets—but unfortunately I have to live by them. I could go on for hours explaining the problems here. Our magazine is printed in Dayton, Ohio, on a mix of roto and letterpress. Costs of everything have escalated: paper, ink, labor. To get us into the twenty-first century, we have in one year moved into an in-house display typesetting operation which has changed our deadlines and methods of processing copy. We have also had to contend with new forms of advertising and new profit pressures on what we call ad-edit ratios, which on a national average for all consumer magazines in 1979 ran to about 49 percent editorial to 51 percent advertising, as opposed to the reverse 51/49 just six years ago. Why? Because the realities of magazine publishing have put the pressure on publishers—

and given additional pressure to editors to make more meaning-
ful statements on smaller canvases.

What does this all do to editors? First of all, it only affects the
senior editors, because it is my feeling that down the line creative
people do not have to know every financial detail, unless they are
burningly ambitious and have desire to find out. Somehow, the
only time most editorial people want to know about the state of
the union is before salary review. And there's a whole other set
of management headaches, by the way.

The problem at the top is keeping it all in place, managing the
management. I frankly did not start out in life wanting to be a
businesswoman. I've become one defensively. I can't get more
pages for my magazine or raises for my staff without financial
know-how. Now I even enjoy the business activities as a challenge. If I were to come back again in another life, I might even
choose to be a corporate chieftain and buy up interesting and
profit-potential companies. But never can I forget that the reason I am where I am is because of the essential talents that got
me there—and they are on the creative side.

It is the duty of an editor-in-chief to produce a consistent,
strong, highly focused editorial product that will stand for something in its readers' lives.

It is the responsibility of an editor-in-chief to produce a magazine that maintains a strong relationship between its editors and
readers. This, of course, requires an understanding of these
readers—their changing lives, needs, and tastes—and a commitment to serve them.

It is the assignment of an editor-in-chief to know every aspect
of the magazine; literally to read (and sometimes revise) every
layout, headline, and illustration; to work with all the top editors
in maintaining consistency of approach, continuity of service,
and high level of news and excitement; to spend seventeen hours
a day (seven for such necessities as food and sleep) in the pursuit
of excellence for that magazine.

Now, how does an editor-in-chief manage to do all that, work
on financial reports, occasionally go out to dinner and the
theater with a spouse or companion, and also find time for
herself?

That's where the real management comes in. And I know from the shared experiences of many women executives that it requires a fantastic amount of juggling.

I know because of friends, and also because in my travels I have appeared on numerous panels with women communicators in all media.

At the *Journal*, in our service to half our audience—women who work—we also have participated in many seminars and studies. Our most recent, reported in the May 1980 issue of the magazine, *Ladies' Home Journal* and the American Telephone and Telegraph Company (AT&T) were cosponsors of perhaps the most in-depth meeting on Women in the Work Force ever held. One hundred thirty men and women in government, education, labor, and national organizations gathered together to discuss many subjects from occupational segregation and two-worker families to opportunity and management for women in the eighties.

Many of the findings from that seminar are relevant here. For example, George Ball, president of E. F. Hutton, seemed to sound a warning to ambitious women when he said, "Quite frankly, I don't think you can be a balanced individual and get to the top in business. It's more than a question of juggling family and career. If you're going to be at the top of a corporation, you are going to be by definition an eccentric, and you'll have to put in seventy- to eighty-hour weeks."

His remarks drew headlines like "Women Hear That Success is Costly," and indeed it is. But just as men manage their lives to accommodate families, hobbies, and civic concerns—not to mention golf—so women can learn to manage their lives. Some of this can be done by zigging-and-zagging at various points in the life cycle: perhaps easing off at the period when children are infants and then coming back—not always easy, but then who said life was easy?

It is important for all of us that some of us do succeed. Said Florence R. Skelly, executive vice-president of the research firm Yankelovich, Skelly and White, "There is no quicker way to ensure that women in general move ahead than to have women already at the top." How are we doing? According to figures the

Yankelovich firm has compiled, there has been a 70 percent increase in the ranks of women managers, as opposed to a 17 percent increase among men in similar jobs. But the figures behind the percentages are not so encouraging when you look at them closely. Two million women are holding jobs that could be described as managerial (and that includes managing the mail room) while ten million men, or five times as many, are so classified.

Many at the conference, by the way, believed that women are being held back by the attitudes of men in power. These traditionalists, in the words of one participant, will "have to be dragged kicking and screaming into the twenty-first century." But others spoke of more educated managements. Carla Hills, former secretary of housing and urban development, summed up: "There's no question that collaboration will serve our purpose better, in today's climate, than confrontation."

But it somehow all reverts back to self-management. I am not going to hold myself up as the model for superorganization. I probably hold the gold cup for a piled-high, seemingly sloppy desk—but believe me, that's what works for my multi-interest methods. I organize to get more time in my life, and I find it by being a perfectionist in selected areas and more relaxed, even casual, in others. I take my responsibilities seriously, including the financial ones, but I know that for my job, zest and initiative and a sense of exploration are possibly more important than some of the mundane chores. I do delegate, probably not enough, but sufficiently so that other people will handle work better than I do.

I have learned patience, compromise, and the gentle art of evasion if delay is important to a decision. These are not new talents for women: they've always had them. A harder lesson to learn is how to stand toe to toe in battle with a confident male, particularly if the battle is in his territory. I no longer act affronted, belittled, or at a disadvantage. I stick to the facts, figure out my opponent's game plan, and try to beat him at his own game. I've even added words like *game plan* to my lexicon, as uncomfortable as that word was at first.

But as editor-in-chief, I can never lose the spark and the spirit and the desire to stir up the same enthusiasm in our staff. That's the tough one, when the crunch is on and there's a transit strike and my husband is having career troubles of his own and the world, at best, seems surly, unreasonable, and headed for new upheavals.

That's when *real* management comes in.

That's when women have to prove their mettle and their fortitude. They have to believe in themselves and the objectives to which they have given their energies. They have to believe in their jobs and their products. On a larger basis, they have to be committed to our form of government and a capitalistic economy. It also helps to believe in the power of faith and application over events. This has nothing to do with dogma: it has to do with daily living and coping. I wish more management courses included how to handle defeats and dark days, and how to move from negative to positive without lying to yourself.

Perhaps these are lessons that cannot be taught.

Perhaps they are only learned on the job, by people who never show their scars but who keep on going—and striving.

At any rate, that to me is the core of management and communication in media, and in any other sector of endeavor.

FOUR

Challenges for Women
in Government Management

Barbara Franklin

Currently a Senior Fellow at the University of Pennsylvania's Wharton School, Barbara Franklin became commissioner of the U.S. Consumer Product Safety Commission when the agency was first created by Congress in 1973; twice she was elected the commission's vice-chairman. Until February 1979 she served with this body as senior commissioner and was known for her interest in assessing the impact of regulation and in unifying the approach to the causes and prevention of cancer.

Prior to her appointment to the Product Safety Commission, Ms. Franklin served as a presidential assistant, in which role she launched the first aggressive White House program to recruit women for top government policy-making positions.

A graduate of Pennsylvania State University (and the youngest recipient of its distinguished alumnus award), Ms. Franklin was one of the first American women to receive an MBA from the Harvard Graduate School of Business Administration; she also holds an honorary Doctor of Science degree from Bryant College in Rhode Island. Among the boards of directors of which she is a member, those of the Aetna Life and Casualty Company and the American Institute of CPAs are notable.

The beginning of the eighties is a very appropriate time to assess the opportunities for women, the environment in which women will be operating, and the role women will play.

Expectations about the role of women in the government and throughout our society have changed dramatically during the seventies. To illustrate, I'll recount my favorite White House experience. I had been working there only a few weeks when a certain gentleman, who should remain nameless, invited me to a luncheon. He introduced me to a predominantly male audience as "Barbara Franklin, the president's new recruit for women," and he said, "I am pleased to tell you she's wearing a bra." I was too flabbergasted to ask him how he knew.

The point is this: that was 1971 and now is 1980. I do not think anyone would dream of introducing a woman, in any context, that way today. It's a measure of the attitude change that has taken place. The governmental and political processes, since I've been in Washington, have become more accessible to women. More women ran for public office in 1979 than had ever been candidates before. Today there are approximately eighteen thousand women holding public office throughout the country. That is double the number from 1975. There are two women governors, who were elected on their own, and not on their husband's, merits. (One of them, Ms. Dixy Lee Ray in the state of Washington, was recruited by me for the Atomic Energy Commission in 1972.) There are a woman senator and several women mayors who gained their positions based on their qualifications. The elective arena is truly beginning to change.

We also note that there have been dramatic increases in the numbers of women in appointed positions throughout the federal government. The past decade has brought changes in the numbers of women who are secretaries, under secretaries, assistant secretaries, and commissioners. Many more women in the career Civil Service have opportunities to move up the career Civil Service ladder. During my White House days, we had the first women who became secret service agents, F.B.I. agents, forest rangers, and helicopter pilots. The numbers are increasing each day.

It has been interesting to watch the role of political wives through the years and note the changes that have occurred during the seventies. These women used to be seen and not heard. But in 1976 people were wearing buttons that said "Elect Betty Ford's Husband." More recently, look at the role played by Mrs. Carter as another example of how things have changed.

Recall the celebrated firing of Bella Abzug from the President's Advisory Commission on Women. It was a front page news story all over the country. There was great speculation about its impact on the political scene. Interesting to note that not so long ago this event would hardly have made the news at all, and where it was noticed it would have been a cause for laughter. This is a stunning illustration of the seriousness of women's political clout.

In viewing the business environment, we see that half of our work force today are women. Many more are starting their own businesses, too; and organizations to represent them, such as Women Business Owners, have been organized. The number of women attending business schools has also increased as the importance of a sound academic background in management increases.

Generally, women have moved ahead in sports; Billie Jean King's beating Bobby Riggs is one example.

We have celebrated International Women's Year, founded women's banks, and joined networks.

These are just some of the indications of change in the roles that women play in our country.

Clearly we still have a long way to go. Our world is not yet perfect when 11 percent of elected offices are held by women and women comprise 53 percent of the electorate. Three hundred women on corporate boards aren't enough when you consider that women own 43 percent of the publicly traded stock. Just because half of the labor force is women doesn't mean that women have an equal chance for promotion and good pay. Women who own their own businesses have a tougher time getting financing for those businesses, and all of us still have to juggle both career and home responsibilities more than men do. We still have to be superwomen.

But clearly many gains have been made, and of greater

significance in this country is the idea that women should have equal status and opportunity. The concept has arrived, and therefore so have we. A recent Harris poll indicates that Americans favor efforts to improve the status of women, 65 percent to 28 percent. In 1970 it was 42 percent for and 41 percent against. That's a sharp increase in just a few years. Our aspirations, as women, our dreams, our needs, our conflicts, our angers, and our sensitivities are out in the open and being taken seriously as never before.

At the same time women have been making these strides, let us consider what has happened to government. First, there was Watergate and the climate of distrust, anxiety, and cynicism it created.

Second, a clear antiregulatory sentiment arose which was directed at government. In my former position as a commissioner on the Consumer Product Safety Commission, I felt the impact of that very personally and directly. Toward the end of the seventies, it was clear to me that the people in this country had had enough of government interfering too much in their businesses and in their lives, and they had had enough of too much paperwork, too many bureaucrats, too much bungling, and too much cost.

Third, there is articulation of the concern that government is not managed well. The word *managed* is being used, where previously it was not. Now, what was described before as inefficiency, bungling, or incompetency is being cast in terms of management. And the government is criticized for its lack of management skill.

What does all this mean? It means to me that the strides women have made toward being taken seriously, toward becoming educated, toward acquiring new kinds of experiences and responsibilities have occurred at a time when government is mistrusted and recognized to need more management skills. There is, then, a great opportunity now for women to bring some of their new experience, new understanding, and new skill to an arena that really needs it.

Let me cite an example of the sort of thing that happens in government and why management is needed there. I remember in the early days of the Consumer Product Safety Commission receiving a briefing package on which the commissioners were to vote. That document was several inches thick and included sections from a variety of disciplines—epidemiology, engineering, law, and economics. The missing element was the integration of the data so that it made sense for regulatory decision-making. Assembling data so that it can be acted upon is very basic. But government is filled with specialists, people who are often very competent with their own material but who lack the managerial skill to bring information together in a cohesive fashion.

Additionally, government needs expertise in planning, setting and implementing goals, and motivating people. In short, management.

There are two general types of jobs in government. There are approximately three million career Civil Service people. The briefing package described earlier is prepared by members of this group. They have tenure in government and often spend their whole working lives there. Within the career Civil Service, management skills are very much needed. Some recent Civil Service reform is intended to provide more incentive for those few who are managers.

Beyond this group is a thin layer of people on top who are political appointees. I had one of these positions, a somewhat unusual one because commissioners in independent agencies have fixed terms. Still, they are political appointees, since they are nominated by the president and confirmed by the Senate. These people in the government—several thousand in number—come and go as administrations change. Management skills are as needed among the political appointees as they are among the civil servants. We have put too many lawyers into these jobs: and while they may be excellent people, they aren't trained in management. (I have made this statement before and been criticized for it, by lawyers.)

What is needed are more people from Cabinet secretaries to assistant secretaries to chairpersons of regulatory commissions who have management expertise. Here is another opportunity for women with management interests and skills.

It can be said especially of business and government, of labor and government, and of consumer activists and government, that these combinations assume an adversarial posture. An illustration from my days with the Consumer Products Safety Commission will reinforce my statement. In 1973 there was clear consensus by consumers, consumer groups, government, and business that a mandatory safety standard for power lawnmowers was needed. The effort began that year and is continuing today seven years later. You ask, what could take seven years? Part of the problem is the antagonistic stance taken by the several interested parties. The consumer group charged with drafting the standard angered the industry representatives and vice versa. The government did not offer proper leadership, and the industry embarked upon a very expensive campaign to discredit whatever proposal evolved from the process. The problem then was a severe lack of communication. This is still evident today but to a lesser degree, and there are indications that a reasonable document will result from the effort.

But in the interim there's been acrimony and wasted time and money, both taxpayers' dollars and industry funds. Of greater importance is the fact that there has not been protection for consumers.

This overly adversarial, time-wasting behavior should stop. I think women can help, capitalizing on the traditional ways many of us have been brought up. Women are often more willing to find ways to accommodate different interests and bring people together to solve problems. Women have a special contribution to make in creating a new era for business and government to work together in our country's interest.

I believe that to a certain extent women have special competencies. Some of these are the result of upbringing but many others—those which may be identified as management skills—are learned through education and experience. Communication skill is an area where I think women excel. This can be capitalized on to build some bridges between business and government.

There are many of us (women) and of them (men) who like Pogo ask, "Who is the government?" The answer, in an oversimplified fashion, is that government is people who do the little

nitty-gritty, everyday bookkeeping for the rest of us. If it weren't
for us in businesses, government wouldn't exist, and we—that is,
we women—would be doing that nitty-gritty bookkeeping.

On the career level there have always been women doing the
little clerical stuff. When the time came to bring in managers to
tame the bureaucracy, the consultants from the big corporations
were men. This is changing, as the government realizes that
management is skill derived rather than a function of maleness,
and further that management as an ability is to be valued,
searched out, and educated for. I see now more career bureaucrats being sent to management schools.

The path, then, for women who have an inclination for government service is becoming less cluttered: and with the changing climate, the opportunities for those of us with management
skills are vastly improved. We have opportunities to do jobs effectively and rise within the bureaucracy far better than we could
have ten years ago.

A word of caution, however: managing in the public arena is
more difficult in some ways than managing in the private sector
because there are more variables to consider in the decision-
making process. These variables include the Congress, the press,
and a whole variety of special interest groups that make their
views known. This is not to say that decisions are made based on
factors other than the merits of the situation, but that the determination must be reviewed in light of the needs of the concerned parties.

Our concern to this point has been directed toward professional awareness. Is it a "velvet" job you seek or avoid? Finding
"velvet" is easy, but it will mark you. You must make a career
goal of avoiding that kind of position, and one sound way is
through a working commitment to education and training.

You might need an MBA, but you will undoubtedly require
on-the-job experience. There are some things that you will not
know how to do, that games and simulations cannot teach. There
are mistakes you will have to make so that you will learn from
them. This process is an ongoing one and provides the
groundwork and professionalism that will carry you through the
tough situations.

What, too, will be your personal needs with regard to work time, flex-time, and condensed work weeks? While many organizations are willing to structure their work schedules to accommodate the needs of their employees, you will have to know and make known your priorities, and when necessary negotiate with someone who is willing to bargain. You will not necessarily find the opportunity to arrange your schedule; and if you can't, you'll have to think through the tradeoffs to be made.

If, for example, you decide to work three days a week or to take five years off, what are you going to give up on the career side? Does it matter to you? On the other hand, if you concentrate heavily on the professional side, what are you giving up personally and is that what you want to do?

The question of how we balance our lives among professional and personal activities is crucial. There are no workable models. Each of us has to find her own answers. This to me is the great challenge women now have. Many opportunities have opened up professionally. It's the personal side that now raises so many questions. How do we accept professional responsibility while still carrying out all the other roles women continue to have to play? Are some changes needed, either in the roles or in the institutions where we work? We have to concentrate on balancing our professional and private lives without having to be super-women.

In summary, women have made many gains in many ways during the last decade. Perhaps this has happened so quickly that we can scarcely comprehend how much change has occurred. But the climate, the environment in which we are pursuing our activities has changed dramatically. The eighties present a particular opportunity for women to capitalize upon: to make changes in the total environment and to move ahead in ways we might never have dreamed possible.

I see government as an area in need of improvement. It needs management, among both political appointees and career people. It needs improved communication with business and a restoration of its credibility; women, as one of the great resources of our country, could begin to fill these needs.

There is a quote that I have enjoyed over the years from

Elizabeth Cady Stanton, who said in 1888, "We feel a peculiar tenderness for the young women on whose shoulders we are about to leave our burdens." Today, almost one hundred years later, it's much less a burden we're getting as women than it is an opportunity and a challenge. How each of us chooses to confront the challenge and capitalize on the opportunity is in our hands as never before.

FIVE

The Decision to Become
Politically Involved

Mary Anne Krupsak

*In November 1974 Mary Anne Krupsak became the first woman to be
elected lieutenant governor of New York State; she had formerly served in
both the New York State Assembly and the New York State Senate for a
total of fourteen years. Ms. Krupsak holds honorary degrees from Boston
University, Clarkson College, and Russell Sage College.*

Politicians, particularly those of us who have had legal training,
tend to favor the development of a topic through a historical
perspective. This empirical route lends itself to the expansion of
this theme: why and how does a woman find herself in a political
situation? Book 17 in the Old Testament is the Book of Esther. A
reading of chapter 2 tells us that Esther was selected as queen.
She didn't have much choice, but queen she was—and as such
she saved her people from annihilation.

The Queen of Sheba is another woman who found herself in

51

the political forefront. Her liaison with Solomon continued her empire's prosperity.

Several centuries later in France, the Maid of Orleans, Joan of Arc, came onto the political scene. Her end was tragic, but the message she carried and her name live on to this day.

In more recent times, we have had other queens—Isabella of Spain, Juliana of the Netherlands, and Elizabeth and Victoria of England—leading their respective countries through hazardous times. These women inherited their political roles.

Other women had a choice, however: Ghandi of India, Meir of Israel, and Thatcher of England. These women were elected to office, rather than having been selected or having come to it through religious calling or through bloodlines.

I can identify with the elected women as this is the route I had to follow, not being of royal blood or chosen. While there are, I'm certain, similarities in women's reasons for seeking public office, there are also many differences, depending upon the individual.

One point I must make very strongly is that you don't, some Sunday afternoon, decide to run for public office because it seems like a nice thing to do. Your resolve to become involved has to be the result of your thinking and feeling a commitment to accomplish a goal or goals for society.

The decision to become an elected offical was, for me, a case of evolution rather than an initial stated purpose. I come from Amsterdam, New York, a small upstate town, very much like many other towns in Massachusetts and around the country. My first exposure to public problems was gained through volunteer work. As I gained broader knowledge of the environment, I developed certain feelings about the problems I saw and began to visualize very broad solutions to the difficulties confronting my community and the state. It became apparent that these issues were not confined to a state or a region, but were national.

I also recognized that it was more feasible and practical at the onset to attempt to solve difficult questions on a small scale rather than attack them on a national level. I ran, was elected to, and served in both houses of the New York State legislature and was finally sent by the voters to Albany as lieutenant governor.

I made the office of lieutenant governor into a focal point for a regional analysis of New York State's strengths, assets, and business growth potential—in short, for opportunities. It was, I felt, the time, place, and position to do something about the problems I saw and the goals I had set for myself to aid society.

Some of the issues I saw revolve around some fundamental facts: One of every two marriages is ending in divorce. One out of every six households in the United States is headed by a woman. Women strive to gain "equal pay for equal work." Women are stuck in occupational ghettos, so-called "female jobs" that are relatively low in pay and prestige. On a larger scale, our country's foreign policy directed to an advocacy for human rights has a credibility problem when we have a double standard for different people.

Many times solutions to problems can be suggested or found by examining history. As an example, during World War II women replaced men effectively at all levels of employment. "Rosy the Riveter" built tanks and battleships. How many women today are involved in the heavy construction trades? Of greater significance, however, are the circumstances that permitted Rosy to work. Probably the greatest assist that all the Rosys had was that, if they had small children, employers provided day-care centers and work periods were altered to permit part-time employment. These were only two things that were done.

Today our work force is larger, but so is our production. We are manufacturing different products and providing services ranging from simple to complex. Our marketplace is world wide, but so is our competition. However, we cannot say that there is nothing to be done for our unemployed, underemployed, and badly employed populations. Government and business must form a partnership, informally and formally, to seek out and find solutions.

As I have been a feminist for many years, my concerns are directed toward the problem of women. Whether we seek employment because of marital status or inflation or in an attempt to improve our living standard, ways have to be found or developed to accommodate us.

Another reason compelling me to enter public life was that

shortly after I received my undergraduate degree, I became aware that I was earning 57 cents for every dollar earned by a man.

I believe that the phrase "equal pay for equal work" should be altered to "equal pay for work of comparable value." The problem of course is twofold: first to define "comparable value" and then to see that women are suitably educated and trained to produce this level of work. With reference to the latter, it is obvious that without access to the requisite skills many of us will never be able to attain equal status. Therefore, our educational system must react to this problem; federal and state legislation should provide the education needed.

Earlier I mentioned two ways that working conditions were altered to permit women to aid in the war effort (day-care centers and part-time schedules). In addition, such concepts as flex-time, compressed work week, and shared work should be thought about, discussed, and implemented.

I believe that opportunities exist to change our work style; but without concerted efforts by the various forces that must interact to produce results, we will continue with a static situation.

When I lost my bid for reelection, I took a long hard look at what I believed in and what I felt. My enthusiasm for societal change had not diminished; I felt I had a new and different opportunity to work toward my goals. This thinking led me to form my own law firm in Albany. We practice general law. However, our focus is toward the development of businesses and the expansion of job opportunities.

Politics is moving from one point to another. It requires a force, someone working in the legislature on some committee or private citizens agitating for change, bringing issues to the attention of elected officials and the electorate. The movement from a thought to a law may be slow and erratic; but if society is to be the beneficiary, then those of us who are willing and able to sustain the concept must eventually succeed.

I believe that the political arena, like any other stage, has room for a large group of diversified players. I encourage you to pursue your goals for elected office and your goals for society.

SIX

Women's Role
in the Private Sector
in Investments

Julia M. Walsh

*Julia M. Walsh is the chairman of the investment firm Julia M. Walsh &
Sons, Inc., which she founded in 1977. Prior to that, she served as vice-
chairman of Ferris and Company, having begun there as a general partner and later having advanced to senior vice-president. She is on the
board of such major corporations as Pitney Bowes.*

*The first woman accepted and graduated from the Advanced Man-
agement Program at the Harvard Graduate School of Business, Ms.
Walsh is the director or member of nine national organizations. She holds
similar positions with eight educational institutions, including Simmons
College, where she is chairman of the board of the Advisory Committee to
the Graduate Program in Management.*

She was a 1945 magna cum laude *graduate of Kent State University and was awarded an honorary DBA at Simmons in 1979.*

Events during the past few years have made some very dramatic changes in everyone's lives, and I don't see the rate of these changes slowing down in any degree that would be identifiable. To the contrary, I see the whole impact of change in our lives speeding up, with more complexity and more difficulty and more challenge but with greater rewards, satisfaction, and opportunity as counterbalancing forces. I want to refer in a very realistic way to the economic factors and their impact on us as individuals; their impact on us as career people, as investors, and most of all as citizens. I think that we are facing a different kind of challenge as women than that which we faced during the past few years. I find it an interesting challenge. I find opportunities that we did not have a decade ago, opportunities that we must not only accept when they are handed to us but must seek out and develop.

It's been a great pleasure for me to have had the opportunity to go to Harvard and now to be involved with Simmons' Graduate Program in Management and to be identified from time to time as one of the more well-known entrepreneurs (I'll use that word as the best description, because there are so few women with that status). My comments, therefore, are presented in the latter context. What are the opportunities? What's ahead for us in the entrepreneurial area? I believe, as a great many sociologists do, that there will be a return to the era of small business in the next twenty years based on economic developments both here and abroad.

Part of this is brought about by changes in the economy, but we also have to be very careful to identify that part of this is brought about by changes in the work force in the United States. As recently as a decade ago the opportunities for women in business were very, very limited; that has changed drastically and significantly.

We have to look at a primary reason for this change if we're interested in any relationship to business and to the educational investment made by women. Allow me to project and predict a little bit about the demographics in the next decade and their impact on those of you who are potential students, undergraduate students or graduate students. We note that by 1990,

53 percent of the entire American work force will be between the ages of 25 and 44. This is an incredible change in the work force curve related to historic precedent since the Second World War. We can anticipate some serious problems as a result.

This shift is a reflection of the post–World War II baby boom and also a reflection of an increase in minorities—women particularly—who have entered the work force in the business arena. Those typical careers that we accepted as normal for women twenty to thirty years ago not only have lost some of their appeal for economic reasons, but also have become overcrowded because of population increases. Business has become one of the last strongholds for big, and unusual, opportunities.

That statistic will also cause tremendous pressures for the expansion of career development programs. Much has been readily available to us in the sixties and the seventies. However, there will be a need for education to be different in the future. I think it's interesting to note that in the past two decades there has been a sixfold increase in the number of MBAs graduating from colleges in the United States. Again, that's part of the emphasis on business and also a broadening of the availability of that type of education to include women and minorities.

Whereas women of my generation were successful in a limited sense with a general education, this will no longer suffice. It's now a necessity to specialize; expertise has to give you some particular special contribution to make to the group that you intend to serve. This has brought about a whole new influx of people into law, accounting, data processing, and other very finite areas.

Some of these fields may require a master's degree to ensure employment and career growth. I think it's important for women to understand that the master's degree itself is not necessarily the *function* requirement so much as it is a *credential* requirement. We are finding that in the olden days—which were five years ago—a bachelor's degree seemed to be adequate to obtain initial employment; chances are it still is. However, the competition today is such that it is no longer adequate from a credential point of view.

As a result of seeing this trend developing in the early seventies, Simmons College saw the need to accommodate a large

number of women who had not been permitted to participate in
the business marketplace, and they inaugurated the Graduate
Program for Women in Management in 1974. Since then, this
program has provided an outstanding opportunity for women
who want to obtain their master's degree quickly, efficiently, and
effectively. Simmons graduates are then able to move out into
the marketplace and use their degrees to the best possible advantage. I think the same can be said for the undergraduate management programs at Simmons. These in many, many ways have
been very much ahead of their time.

Unfortunately, however, there are few educational institutions
ready and able to educate women. We must, then, accept that if
we intend to pursue careers in business, in the economy, in government, in federal institutions, and even in education (because
the educational society has become so deeply involved in the business arena), then we are going to have to put our minds to the
task and set about, in a much different way than we have in the
past, to organize our efforts to best accommodate the future.

One of the problems that we're seeing to a great extent among
women students and women career people is that we have not
been accurately conditioned to think in terms of the economic
impact on us as a group and as individuals. I say *conditioned,* not
educated. I think we are as well educated as the rest, but we have
not been really introduced to thinking systematically about our
relationship to the economy and how we adapt to it: how we
manage our cash, how we save, whether or not we buy a home,
how we provide for our children's education. A great deal of our
approach to these kinds of problems, for whatever reason, has
been allowed to be haphazard.

It's terribly important that we get to think in terms of the
decision-making processes and an orderly approach to our own
economic viability in a very difficult world. I have been as-
tounded and amazed at the numbers of women (and this I can
attest to as an investment counselor) who have relinquished or
neglected to direct their own activities. They are more concerned
with the affairs and economic standards of others. One of the
most classic remarks heard from extremely successful career
women is "I really don't have time to think about my own situa-

tion." And all too often what is happening is that they are approaching a disastrous economic future in terms of investing, in terms of savings, and in terms of cash management. It is appalling to me that we're allowing this to happen.

Let me refer as a case in point to one of those simple, dramatic, and difficult conditions with which the economy has to deal. The situation is the extremely high cost of money in today's environment.

I want to separate this issue from other considerations. Certainly one can't oversimplify the economy in any kind of framework, but we must try to address individual issues if we are to attempt to understand the impact of the cost of money on everything we do.

The most serious thing about the recent market situation in which the prime rate moved up to 20 percent and back down is that the more conservative investors felt the greatest negative impact. It was the conservative investor—the bond buyer, the utility holder, the kind of person who puts his/her money in the safe income producing kinds of revenue, bonds or savings and loan—who was most impacted by this economic development. The most serious implication was that people did not consider the long-term impact.

It is terribly important when we're in a very difficult economic environment, as we are now (and I don't think it's going to get easier for quite a while), that we learn how to adapt and live with it as comfortably as possible. And the fact of the matter is that it is not very comfortable at the moment.

What we're finding, and what I want you to think about as we begin to move through the next decade, is that people are reacting instead of acting. It is a difficult problem. We are more prone to react and therefore find ourselves, oftentimes, very much more seriously penalized than we would have been had we acted instead of reacted. Therefore, the intelligent and prudent posture to assume is that of "planner." If you have some accounting background, financial planning will be easier. But you should learn how to do a cash flow and to project how you can best insulate yourself against negative conditions. You are never going to be able to internalize an intelligent approach to your own financial plan and independence unless you yourself are doing it and getting the experience of doing it.

I referred earlier to economic conditioning. I really am very anxious to find a way to get this included in business education for women so that it becomes a more natural part of our thinking.

I've watched my daughters growing and learning. They're doing some very fun things, in and with their education. I've tried to make them think in terms of reality, not women-related reality, but economic-related reality. And frankly, the economic education doesn't change because they're female—although it may if they're fortunate enough to marry a rich man. I find that probably one of the best solutions to economic problems. But certainly it is not one which is guaranteed and is also subject to change. It is a form of "relaxing," not controlling or participating. Participation means dealing with economics on a family level. I've often wondered why this has not been a more natural state. I could understand it for my generation or possibly for people in their forties, but for those in their thirties there are no excuses anymore. A woman in her twenties should be head and shoulders above everyone else in long range plans and ask herself, What am I doing? and How am I preparing myself to have this an integral part of my thinking process? And she'll find, if she asks around, that not many women do.

The crucial issue for me in economic education is the risk/ reward ratio. I have very strong feelings about risk/reward, but I really didn't know what I was talking about until I took my big risk and went off in business for myself. Now I knew, or thought I knew, what the risks and the rewards were. But I, like most other women in my age group, was reacting instead of acting. When I chose to act in '77, I found that I hadn't really understood very well what the risk/reward ratio was, the kinds of responsibilities people have to take when they evaluate risk in a realistic way.

Three years will have passed since I founded Julia Walsh & Sons. My team is made up of four very well-qualified, very well-equipped boys who just happen to be my sons. There is a togetherness about our organization. We aren't dealing with strangers and the mutuality of interests is great.

However, while we have some fun in our work, we also have found out about risks and entrepreneurship. We did a study on the Dow recently and recorded its up and down movement. Our findings indicate that there has been more movement in the Dow since we've been in business than there had been in total in the last twenty years. That's the degree of volatility in the marketplace today, relative to previous times. The risk/reward ratio is something that we really learn to live with.

I indicated earlier that the most serious impact of this recent market has been that the conservative investor has taken the greatest amount of risk. These investors gave up, sacrificed, potential reward to avoid risk. They did this without an assured reward factor, thereby taking a greater risk than most other investors. Now what does this mean? I think it means that it is very important that you understand the difference between risk and reward, that you understand what risk really is. And it is dealt with in a very different way than we've dealt with it in the past.

You have to set about developing, possibly in graphic form, what minimal rewards you will accept for the risks you have to take. Then set about determining which form of investment generates the best reward for you. I believe sincerely that the ownership of American industry will continue to be the greatest single opportunity for investors available anywhere. Now you may say real estate? Of course real estate. It's been extremely exciting. And if you say, purchasing your own home, I say, "Bravo." Because that has all kinds of implications above and beyond financial implications. It has tax implications, but more than that it has happiness and satisfaction implications beyond material value. But it's terribly important that you understand and learn to deal with investing in equity, real estate equity or securities equity. I contend that in the next few years the intelligent investor will be more rewarded than any time since the late fifties. Now how can I be so sure of this? If one looks at the three major problems we're dealing with, we can see they have gelled since the decade of the sixties.

The three problems I refer to should be obvious. First, there is *our international relationships*. The United States did have the world to itself for a long time, and had to adjust in the late sixties as our competition came into more real confrontation with us.

We had to face up to the *overevaluation of the dollar,* which has caused some very difficult economic implications internationally. We also had to learn to live with the cost of money and inflation which has really plagued us and still presents a serious problem, one which is not easily solved. The third thorn in our national side is *the energy problem.* Controls within the nation caused us to become unbelievably at the mercy of oil-producing nations. I believe this will change. We will move slowly, painfully, and not always on an even keel toward a solution to the energy supply problem.

The current thinking in our country tends to be negative toward a solution of the energy crisis. I can understand that, but we can observe a movement toward a much more open marketplace for oil and gas, toward some technological change, toward a situation where we are more competitive in prices. We have to remember that there is no shortage of oil and gas in the world. The crisis is rather a function of the price people are willing to pay versus the price being asked. We are going to approach the oil and gas situation from the point of view of supply and also in terms of changing the demand and subsequent consumption of energy.

If you have money to invest, or if you don't have, you should begin to accumulate, and view the securities market in a different way based upon my analysis of the aforementioned problems. One of the problems of investment is that traditional habits tend to dominate a realistic appraisal of where opportunity lies.

Another factor which may not be a major problem for many of you yet, but hopefully will be a very serious problem in the future, is the problem of taxation. Taxes are always a nice problem because it means you're making lots of money. It's very painful, however, when you have to pay them. Taxation should be part of your overall financial planning. How do you deal with taxation? How do you best protect in an intelligent way as much of your income as you possibly can for future use? Here I suggest that many of you are not looking at other opportunities. You're not building an investment program with your long-range tax implications in place.

The bulk tax factor today still is the long-term capital gain. So why is investing an opportunity to meet that tax challenge? It is because it reveals other long-term opportunities: opportunities for direct investment in oil and gas; opportunities in real estate syndications and public kinds of real estate. But for anyone to omit tax-planning from his/her investment strategy is to court eventual financial tragedy.

I indicated previously that I relished being described as an entrepreneur. It would be helpful, then, to define this word, bringing together some of what I've already stated and leading into the next topic. An entrepreneur is a person who organizes, operates, and assumes the risks and benefits from the rewards in a business. (Notice that we are confronted with risks and rewards again.) My point now is that the thrust of most business schools today for their graduates has been toward involvement with large corporations.

There is nothing wrong with the large corporate environment. For the person who is successful in a large corporation, I say *great*. But returning to my projection of the population in the coming decades (53 percent of the people will be between the ages of 25 and 44), I see that the business arena will be over-populated and that opportunities for entrepreneurship will become infinitely more difficult for the woman attempting to penetrate the large corporate field. Therefore, we must look elsewhere for rewards.

The problem, however, is a compound one. The people who are and will be the most vulnerable, women and minorities, are those who are generally unwilling to assume risks. Why? Basically, this segment of our society has not been introduced to, and been enabled to develop in, the proper tracking of an entrepreneur situation.

We see the government trying to step in and fill the educational, training, and support gap through agencies such as the Small Business Administration. Also, groups like the Greater Washington Minorities Council are working toward similar goals.

Fundamentally, anyone attempting to become an entrepreneur must develop a basic understanding of economic principles and a mature approach to his/her personal financial capability. The absence of either of the foregoing will greatly reduce the chances of survival in the marketplace.

There are also three basic ingredients that go into the makeup of the aspiring businesswoman. These elements are just as important for the woman who will form her own business as for the individual who plans to cast her lot with a large corporation. I feel that these components are equally important and none should be slighted.

The first item is *experience;* and the harder earned, the better. I am very nervous about the individual who attempts to enter the business arena without a practical background and the commensurate understanding of the fundamentals of business. I don't believe that anyone can have an impact as an individual entrepreneur or as a member of a corporate team without "street sense." I certainly do not imply that academic preparation is of lesser value, for it is essential. However, the School of Hard Knocks is equally important.

The second ingredient is *conditioning.* This is one of the most serious deficits that we women have as business people. We have not been taught to act automatically, instinctively, and unemotionally. I'm not saying that we should become computers and be totally unemotional, but rather that our actions and decisions should be the result of rational thinking. I must say, too, that it has been my misfortune to observe the shortcomings in women's attitudes that preclude their facing the realities that exist. Our responsibility as women, to each other and as mothers to our daughters, is to condition, to show and teach, the approaches to logical problem-solving.

Finally, and here it may appear I am returning to an earlier topic, woman need an *understanding of risk.* We must understand that there are no rewards without risk. Hence, not taking a risk is in itself risky, because we will not become eligible for any reward. If we examine and segment a risk into its smallest components, many times we may see that the risk is not too great and therefore is worth taking.

Women have for too long lived in what they perceived as a riskless society, cared for by men: first their fathers, then boyfriends, followed by husbands. It should be clear that this perception of "lack of risk" has led us to the roles referred to as *traditional,* and we women are reaping the negative rewards of this situation. Many of us are now compelled to risk more than we might have to in order to break out of the mold. I contend that we have to change dramatically in the next few years if we want to play in the tough arena of the business world.

I believe also that we will see some very serious backlash over affirmative action. We are going to have to learn to live with it and deal with it; it's going to have to be dealt with in business as well as in general society. The fact that as of this writing the United States as a political entity is reluctant to pass the Equal Rights Amendment is the clearest example.

When I settled in Washington in 1975, I was not one of the women who were bold enough or strong enough or felt strongly enough to go out and fight for the ERA. I was not alone. Other women whose names you may be familiar with assumed the same posture.

Our thinking was that we were living in an enlightened age. So why in the world would anybody in our nation deny women equal rights?

Well, it's five years later and it looks like, at least for this round, a pretty hopeless cause. I believe that this is a form of affirmative action backlash.

Politically you may feel differently about the situation. But I think that realistically our world is not ready to say "Women are equal." If they're not prepared to say it in a political sense, it is unreal to expect a different or more sensitive attitude in the economic area.

Fundamentally I am and will continue to be an optimist. I have learned, however, that an optimistic attitude has to be tempered by realism. I have no problem facing the coming decades. I see difficult times ahead, countless problems and frustrations. But I also see exciting challenges and rewards.

We must face the future knowing that it will be different and fast-paced. Conditions that required decades to evolve twenty or thirty years ago now take only two or three years to mature. Elements impacting one another have produced acute situations such as the Iranian crisis, and this as a new element has gone on causing even greater stresses. Our problem is to recognize and be prepared for violent shifts and serious challenges in a very rapidly moving situation. To do this we must be ready with an educated and emotionally trained population.

To this point, my approach has been microcosmic, dealing with the avenues women should use to gain access to the business world, a world which is essentially within a local community, a state, or possibly the United States. But what of the world?

Enlightened individuals—politicians and corporate leaders—have for some time understood that our country is neither insulated nor isolated from the world community. Conflicts between American businesses and the U.S. government have proven to be serious detriments toward our competing effectively not only with our political allies but also with our political adversaries.

It is time for us (women) to step forward politically, and in any other way in which we can serve, into the international business arena and present the perspectives we have. We can no longer say that this task belongs to others as part of their heritage. If we want to succeed economically, financially, and with our own ambitions, we must be willing to contribute our time and effort toward development of a political consciousness.

I feel very strongly that the next hurdle for us to jump is to move into policy- and decision-making roles that will permit us to impact on the international scene.

How can we do this? Not easily. I must charge those of you who are just starting out with the responsibility, you must start small and you must be recognized as someone who wants to get involved. Join a school committee, political organization, or volunteer group of some kind. Stay aware of your goal and seek out opportunities to see and be seen. Be constructive in your work and conscious of the changing environment locally, nationally, and internationally. Develop a knowledge base of areas contiguous to your professional interests.

I am convinced, as any optimist should be, that involvement eventually produces good results. To state it another way, "Take the risk, there are rewards."

Books in the

Key Issues Lecture Series:

BUSINESS PROBLEMS OF THE SEVENTIES (1973)

Edited by Jules Backman, Research Professor Emeritus of Economics, New York University.

A foreword by Harold S. Geneen, Chairman Emeritus, International Telephone and Telegraph Corporation.

Martin R. Gainsbrugh, formerly Chief Economist, The Conference Board

Solomon Fabricant, Professor of Economics, New York University

C. Fred Bergsten, Senior Fellow, The Brookings Institution

Simon N. Whitney, Visiting Professor of Economics, Baruch College, City University

M. A. Adelman, Professor of Economics, Massachusetts Institute of Technology

Jesse W. Markham, Harvard University, Charles Edward Wilson Professor of Business Administration

Lee Loevinger, Partner, Hogan and Hartson, Attorneys at Law

ADVERTISING AND SOCIETY (1974)

Edited by Yale Brozen, Professor of Business Economics, Graduate School of Business, University of Chicago

A foreword by Harold S. Geneen, Chairman Emeritus, International Telephone and Telegraph Corporation
Daniel J. Boorstin, Smithsonian Institution
Lester G. Telser, University of Chicago
Phillip Nelson, State University of New York at Binghamton
Harold Demsetz, University of California at Los Angeles
Richard A. Posner, University of Chicago
Robert Pitofsky, New York University, Georgetown Law School
John A. P. Treasure, J. Walter Thompson Company
Philip Kotler, Northwestern University

MULTINATIONAL CORPORATIONS, TRADE AND THE DOLLAR (1974)

Edited by Jules Backman and Ernest Bloch, New York University

A foreword by Harold S. Geneen, Chairman Emeritus, International Telephone and Telegraph Corporation
Charles P. Kindleberger, Ford Professor of Economics, Massachusetts Institute of Technology
Raymond Vernon, Herbert F. Johnson Professor of International Business Management, Graduate School of Business Administration, Harvard University
Arnold W. Sametz, Professor of Finance, New York University

LABOR, TECHNOLOGY, AND PRODUCTIVITY (1974)

Edited by Jules Backman, Research Professor Emeritus of Economics, New York University

A foreword by Harold S. Geneen, Chairman Emeritus, International Telephone and Telegraph Corporation
Emanuel Stein, Professor of Economics, Humanities, and Social Sciences, New York University
David L. Cole, Chairman, National Commission for Industrial Peace
Peter F. Drucker, Marie Rankin Clarke Professor of Social Science, Claremont Graduate School, Claremont, California
John W. Kendrick, Professor of Economics, The George Washington University

LARGE CORPORATIONS IN A CHANGING SOCIETY
(1975)

Edited by J. Fred Weston, Professor of Business Economics, Graduate School of Management, University of California, Los Angeles.

A foreword by Harold S. Geneen, Chairman Emeritus, International Telephone and Telegraph Corporation
Oscar Grusky, Professor of Sociology, UCLA
Marc Nerlove, Professor of Economics, University of Chicago
Oliver E. Williamson, Professor of Economics, University of Pennsylvania
Richard A. Posner, Professor of Law, University of Chicago
Sidney M. Robbins, Professor of Finance, Columbia University
Robert B. Stobaugh, Professor of Business Administration, Harvard University
Neil H. Jacoby, Professor of Economics and Policy, Graduate School of Management, UCLA
Michael Granfield, Assistant Professor of Business Economics, Graduate School of Management, UCLA
Ronald H. Coase, Professor of Economics, University of Chicago Law School

SOCIAL RESPONSIBILITY AND ACCOUNTABILITY
(1975)

Edited by Jules Backman, Research Professor Emeritus of Economics, New York University

A foreword by Harold S. Geneen, Chairman Emeritus, International Telephone and Telegraph Corporation
James M. Hester, Rector, the United Nations University, Tokyo, Japan
Juanita M. Kreps, Vice-President and James B. Duke Professor of Economics, Duke University
Oskar Morgenstern, Professor Emeritus of Economics, New York University
Eleanor Bernert Sheldon, President, Social Science Research Council
Robert Parke, Director, Center for Coordination of Research on Social Indicators, Social Science Research Council
David F. Linowes, Partner, Laventhol Krekstein Horwath & Horwath, Worldwide Auditors and Consultants
Harry Schwartz, Visiting Professor of Medical Economics, Faculty of Medicine, Columbia University
Roger G. Kennedy, Vice-President, Ford Foundation
Ingo Walter, Professor of Economics and Finance, New York University

BUSINESS AND THE AMERICAN ECONOMY,
1776–2001 (1976)

Edited by Jules Backman, Research Professor Emeritus of Economics, New York University

A foreword by Harold S. Geneen, Chairman Emeritus, International Telephone and Telegraph Corporation
Solomon Fabricant, Professor Emeritus of Economics, New York University

Carl Kaysen, Director, The Institute of Advanced Study
 Princeton, N.J.
Roger M. Blough, Partner, White & Case
Andrew F. Brimmer, Graduate School of Business Administra-
 tion, Harvard University
Michael Schiff, Professor of Accounting, New York University
John Diebold, Chairman, The Diebold Group

BUSINESS-GOVERNMENT RELATIONS (1976)

Edited by James Wiggins, with a preface by Alan Heslop, Dean
of the Faculty, Claremont Men's College

A foreword by Harold S. Geneen, Chairman Emeritus, Interna-
 tional Telephone and Telegraph Corporation
Herbert Stein, Professor of Economics, University of Virginia
Milton Friedman, Professor of Economics, University of Chicago
Irving Kristol, Professor of Urban Values, New York University
Daniel J. Haughton, former Chairman of the Board, Lockheed
 Aircraft Corporation
William F. Buckley, Jr., Editor, *The National Review*
Walt W. Rostow, Professor of Economics and History, University
 of Texas
Arthur J. Goldberg, former Associate Justice, U.S. Supreme
 Court

ENERGY: THE POLICY ISSUES (1975)

Edited by Gary D. Eppen, Associate Dean and Professor of Industrial Administration, Graduate School of Business, University
of Chicago

A foreword by Harold S. Geneen, Chairman Emeritus, International Telephone and Telegraph Corporation
Robert G. Sachs, Director of Argonne National Laboratory

Barry Commoner, Director of the Center for the Biology of
Natural Systems
Hans J. Morgenthau, City University of New York, Leonard
Davis Distinguished Professor of Political Science
Marvin Zonis, Associate Professor of Behavioral and Political
Science, University of Chicago
M. A. Adelman, Professor of Economics, Massachusetts Institute
of Technology
Robert Z. Aliber, Professor of International Economics and Fi-
nance, Graduate School of Business, University of Chicago
William A. Johnson, Professor of Economics, George Washing-
ton University

THE ECONOMY IN TRANSITION (1976)

Edited by Robert C. Blattberg, Associate Professor of Marketing
Statistics, University of Chicago

A foreword by Harold S. Geneen, Chairman Emeritus, Interna-
tional Telephone and Telegraph Corporation
W. Allen Wallis, Chancellor, University of Rochester
Richard N. Cooper, Frank Altschul Professor of International
Economics, Yale University
William H. Riker, Wilson Professor of Political Science, Univer-
sity of Rochester
Allen H. Meltzer, Maurice Falk Professor of Economics and So-
cial Science, Carnegie-Mellon University
Ezra Solomon, Dean Witter Professor of Finance, Stanford Uni-
versity
Martin Feldstein, Professor of Economics, Harvard University

INTERNATIONAL BUSINESS PROSPECTS,
1977–1999 (1978)

Edited by Howard F. Van Zandt, School of Management and
Administration, University of Texas at Dallas

A foreword by Harold S. Geneen, Chairman Emeritus, International Telephone and Telephone Corporation

Edward T. Hall, Professor of Anthropology, Northwestern University

Sir James Lindsay, Director of International Programmes, International Staff College, United Kingdom

Anthony S. Rojko, Economic Research Service, U.S. Department of Agriculture

John F. Shaw, International Business Counselor and former Director of Far East Operations, North Texas Commission, Commercial Affairs Counselor to U.S. Department of State in Far East

James M. Voss, Chairman of Caltex Petroleum Corporation

William B. Wolf, Professor of Industrial and Labor Relations, Cornell University

David L. Edgell, U.S. Travel Service, Department of Commerce and former Professor at George Washington University

THE WORLD CAPITAL SHORTAGE (1977)

Edited by Alan Heslop, Dean of the Faculty, Claremont Men's College

A foreword by Harold S. Geneen, Chairman Emeritus, International Telephone and Telegraph Corporation

John Lintner, Professor at the Harvard Graduate School of Business Administration

David I. Meiselman, Professor of Economics, Virginia Polytechnic Institute

Geoffrey Bell, Director of J. Henry Schorder Wagg & Company, Ltd. and Columnist for *The Times* of London

Dan Throop Smith, Professor of Finance Emeritus, Harvard University and Senior Research Fellow at Stanford University's Hoover Institution on War, Revolution and Peace

Michael C. Jensen, Professor at the University of Rochester Graduate School of Management

Leon T. Kendall, President and Chief Executive Officer of Mortgage Guaranty Insurance Corporation, Milwaukee, Wisconsin

CHANGING MARKETING STRATEGIES IN A NEW ECONOMY (1977)

Edited by Jules Backman and John A. Czepiel of New York University School of Business and Public Administration

A foreword by Harold S. Geneen, Chairman Emeritus, International Telephone and Telegraph Corporation
Theodore Levitt, Graduate School of Business Administration, Harvard University
Philip Kotler, Harold T. Martin Professor of Marketing, Northwestern University
Arnold Corbin, former President of American Marketing Association and Professor Emeritus of Marketing, New York University
Gerald J. Glasser, Professor of Business Statistics, New York University
Thomas R. Wilcox, Chairman of the Board of Crocker National Bank
J. Fred Bucy, President and Chief Operating Officer, Texas Instruments

ACCOUNTING FOR MULTINATIONAL ENTERPRISES (1978)

Edited by Dhia D. Alhashim and James W. Robertson of California State University of Northridge School of Business Administration and Economics

A foreword by Harold S. Geneen, Chairman Emeritus, International Telephone and Telegraph Corporation

Robert I. Jones, Co-chairman of Arthur Andersen & Company

R. Lee Brummet, Professor of Business Administration, University of North Carolina

Michael N. Chetkovich, Managing Partner of Haskins & Sells and Chairman-elect, American Institute Certified Public Accountants

Ernest L. Ten Eyck, Regional Administrator (Los Angeles), Securities & Exchange Commission

James J. Quinn, National Director of Accounting, Auditing and SEC Practice at Coopers & Lybrand

Lee J. Seidler, Professor of Accounting, New York University

Joseph E. Connor, Jr. Managing Partner — West for Price Waterhouse & Co.

George M. Scott, Associate Professor, University of Texas at Austin

J. Frank Drapalik, Partner, Ernst & Ernst

Hanns-Martin Schoenfeld, Weldon Powell Professor of Accountancy, University of Illinois at Urbana-Champaign

Seymour M. Bohrer, Managing Partner (Los Angeles) of Peat, Marwick, Mitchell & Co.

Robert J. Patrick, Jr., International Tax Counsel and Director, Office of International Tax Affairs, U.S. Treasury Department

Samuel M. Frohlich, Director of International Tax Practice, Arthur Young & Co.

BUSINESS PROBLEMS OF THE EIGHTIES (1980)

Edited by Jules Backman, Research Professor Emeritus of Economics, New York University

A foreword by Harold S. Geneen, Chairman Emeritus, International Telephone and Telegraph Corporation

Lee Loevinger, Partner, Hogan & Hartson, "The Impacts of Government Regulation"

William C. Freund, Senior Vice President and Chief Economist, New York Stock Exchange, "Capital Problems of the 1980s"

Jesse W. Markham, Charles E. Wilson Professor of Business
Administration, Harvard University, "The Changing Nature
of the Marketplace"
Arnold R. Weber, Provost, Carnegie-Mellon University, "The
Changing Labor Market Environment"
Melvyn Krauss, Professor of Economics, New York University,
"Business in the International Environment"
Solomon Fabricant, Professor Emeritus of Economics, New York
University, "The Stagflation Problem"

DEMOCRACY . . . TECHNOLOGY . . . COLLISION!
(1980)

Edited by Dr. Al Paul Klose, Chairman, Department of Communication, Seton Hall University

A foreword by Harold S. Geneen, Chairman Emeritus, Interna-
tional Telephone and Telegraph Corporation
Isaac Asimov, Professor of Biochemistry, Boston University,
"Technology: The Century to the Stars"
Neil Postman, Professor of Media Ecology, New York University,
"Mass Communication: Culture in Crisis"
William F. Buckley, Jr., Author, Editor, Lecturer, "Will Democ-
racy Stave Off '1984'?"
Hon. Kenneth Cox, former FCC Commissioner, "Can the First
Amendment Be Our Guide in the New Technological Era?"
Robert Wussler, President, Pyramid Enterprises Ltd., "Technol-
ogy: The Re-creation of 'Town Hall Democracy'"
George Gerbner, Dean, Annenberg School of Communications,
The University of Pennsylvania, "Electronic Children: Will the
New Generation be Different?"

U.S. AND THE PACIFIC ECONOMY IN THE 1980s
(1980)

Edited by Kermit O. Hanson, Dean of the Graduate School of
Business Administration, University of Washington, and Thomas

W. Roehl, Assistant Professor of International Business, University of Washington

A foreword by Rand V. Araskog, Chairman and President, International Telephone and Telegraph Corporation
Dr. Laurence B. Krause, The Brookings Institution, "The Pacific Economy in an Interdependent World"
Professor Peter D. Drysdale, Australian National University, "Australia's Reorientation Toward the Pacific"
Professor Paul W. Kuznets, Indiana University, "Korea and Taiwan: Implications of Rapid Growth in the Pacific"
Professor Hugh T. Patrick, Economic Growth Center, Yale University, "U.S.–Japanese Political Economy: Is the Partnership in Jeopardy?"
Derek G. Davies, Editor, *Far Eastern Economic Review,* "U.S.–P.R.C. Relationships in the Changing Pacific Context"
Sixto K. Roxas, Vice Chairman, American Express International Banking Corp., President, Bancom Development Corp., Manila, "The Evolving ASEAN Economic Community"
Louis J. Mulkern, Executive Vice President (Retired), Asian Division, Bank of America, "Japan and Asia—Interdependence and Prosperity"

THE BUSINESS BEAT:
ITS IMPACT & ITS PROBLEMS (1980)

Edited by William McPhatter, Director of the Business Journalism Program, University of Missouri School of Journalism

A foreword by Rand V. Araskog, Chairman and President, International Telephone and Telegraph Corporation
Lewis H. Young, Editor-in-chief, *Business Week,* "Business and the Media"
Chris Welles, Author and Freelance Journalist, "Fit or Unfit Business News"
Lewis W. Foy, Chairman, Bethlehem Steel Corporation, "How Business Assesses the Business Press"

Mike Jablonski, Director of Public Relations, TRW, Inc., "PR and
the Business Beat"
Isadore Barmash, Business and Finance Reporter, *The New York
Times,* "The How and the Why of the Business Story"
Dan Cordtz, Senior Economics Editor, ABC Television, "Busi-
ness in Sight and Sound"

WOMEN IN MANAGEMENT: ENVIRONMENT AND ROLE
(1981)

Edited by Dr. Milton L. Shuch, Chairman, Department of Management, Simmons College

A foreword by Rand V. Araskog, Chairman and President, In-
ternational Telephone and Telegraph Corporation
Polly Bergen, Director, The Singer Company, "Blueprint for the
Top Manager—*Me*"
Sylvia Auerbach, former Managing Editor, *Library Journal,* and
Associate Editor, *Publishers Weekly,* "Personal Economics for
Today's Woman"
Lenore Hershey, Editor-in-chief, *Ladies' Home Journal,* "Com-
municating and Managing the Media Challenge"
Barbara Franklin, Senior Fellow, Wharton School, University of
Pennsylvania, "Challenges for Women in Government Man-
agement"
Mary Anne Krupsak, former Lieutenant Governor of New York
State, "The Decision to Become Politically Involved"
Julia M. Walsh, Chairman of the Board, Julia Walsh & Sons, Inc.,
"Women's Role in the Private Sector in Investments"

SOUTHERN BUSINESS: THE DECADES AHEAD (1981)

Edited by David A. Shannon, Vice President and Provost, University of Virginia

A foreword by Rand V. Araskog, Chairman and President, International Telephone and Telegraph Corporation

Sheldon Hackney, President, Tulane University, "The Past as Prologue"

Thomas I. Storrs, Chairman of the Board, NCNB Corporation, "The Southern Economy"

E. Blaine Liner, Executive Director, Southern Growth Policies Board, "The Urbanization of the South"

Richard A. Beaumont, President, Organization Resources Counselors, Inc., "Working in the South"

John Sheldon Reed, Professor of Sociology, University of North Carolina at Chapel Hill, "Grits and Gravy: Observations on the South's New Business and Professional People"

Samuel DuBois Cook, President, Dillard University, "A Humanistic Vision: Beyond Racism and Poverty in the South"

Luther H. Hodges, Jr., Deputy Secretary of Commerce, "The South, the Nation and the World"

REGULATION AND DEREGULATION (1981)

Edited by Jules Backman, Research Professor Emeritus of Economics, New York University

A foreword by Rand V. Araskog, Chairman and President, International Telephone and Telegraph Corporation

Dick Netzer, Dean, Graduate School of Public Administration, New York University, "The Problem of Dismantling Government Regulations"

Murray L. Weidenbaum, Director, Center for the Study of American Business, Washington University, "Saving the Economy by Regulatory Reform"

Yale Brozen, Professor of Business Economics, University of Chicago, "Areas of Increasing Regulation"

Hon. Elizabeth E. Bailey, Member of the Civil Aeronautics Board, "Deregulation of the Airlines: A Case Study"

Hendrik S. Houthakker, Henry Lee Professor of Economics,
   Harvard University, "The Philosophy of Deregulation"
Ernest Bloch, C.W. Gerstenberg Professor of Finance, New York
   University, "Regulation and Deregulation of Financial Institu-
   tions"